JOHN LANCASTER SPALDING

John Lancaster Spalding

THE GABRIEL RICHARD LECTURE

John Lancaster Spalding

FIRST BISHOP OF PEORIA

AMERICAN EDUCATOR

BY

JOHN TRACY ELLIS

PROFESSOR OF CHURCH HISTORY
IN
THE CATHOLIC UNIVERSITY OF AMERICA

1961

THE NATIONAL CATHOLIC EDUCATIONAL ASSOCIATION

THE BRUCE PUBLISHING COMPANY • *Milwaukee*

NIHIL OBSTAT:

Louis A. Arand, S.S.
Censor deputatus

IMPRIMATUR:

Patrick A. O'Boyle
Archbishop of Washington

June 1, 1961

The *nihil obstat* and *imprimatur* are official declarations that a work is free of doctrinal error. No implication is contained therein that those who have granted the *nihil obstat* and the *imprimatur* agree with the content, opinions, or statements expressed.

Library of Congress Catalog Card Number: 62–12433

JOHN LANCASTER SPALDING

John Lancaster Spalding

FIRST BISHOP OF PEORIA
AMERICAN EDUCATOR

"If there is less hostility today, if we, as Catholics, are better understood in the United States, it is largely through the strength and eloquence of his voice."[1] One could hardly ask for a more flattering tribute to his lifework than these words of Peter J. Muldoon, Bishop of Rockford, spoken of John Lancaster Spalding at the testimonial dinner held on November 24, 1913, to honor his golden jubilee as a priest. To have influenced the men of one's own generation in such a way that they see the religious beliefs and practices of their countrymen of other faiths in a new and authentic light, and to have been the instrument through which their prejudices have been dissipated and their errors cleared away, is to have fulfilled one of the highest functions of an educator. That Bishop Spalding merited this praise was evident to all who knew anything about his tireless efforts to make Catholicism rightly understood by his fellow citizens, as well as about his lifelong crusade in behalf of higher educational standards for all Americans. It was, perhaps, the characteristic by which he was most frequently identified in the minds of his contemporaries. Thus, eleven years before his fiftieth anniversary as a priest, when notables of Church and State gathered on May 1, 1902, to commemorate his silver jubilee as a bishop, the preacher of the day, James Cardinal Gibbons, Archbishop of Baltimore, struck the same note. "The splendid talents with which God has endowed you," said the cardinal, "have been employed not only in instructing the faithful of your own diocese, but also in enlightening your fellow citizens throughout the land."[2]

Festive occasions of this kind often prompt friends and admirers to exaggerated statements concerning a jubilarian's achievements. Yet the tributes of Gibbons and Muldoon would have been endorsed by most Americans of that time who had followed the career of the first Bishop of Peoria. It is important, therefore, for an understanding of Spalding's role as an educator to determine at the outset as accurately as one can what were the chief formative factors in his training that prepared him to play so competently the role in which his life was cast. The first was clearly the uplifting influence of the Spalding home. Born on June 2, 1840, at Lebanon, Kentucky, the oldest of the nine children of Richard Martin Spalding and Mary Jane Lancaster, from the beginning Spalding had the advantage of membership in two Catholic families

2

whose more than average abilities showed in colonial Maryland as well as during Kentucky's earliest years as a frontier settlement and state. Originally the Spaldings had migrated to America from Lincolnshire in England, and they were established in St. Mary's County, Maryland, before 1650. By the time of his birth, therefore, Spalding's paternal ancestors had been upon American soil for nearly two centuries, and the Lancasters were likewise long resident in Maryland before the first of their number sought a new home in Kentucky in 1788.

It is easy to attach undue importance to the length of time that a man's ancestors have been resident in the United States, or in any other country. But the relative antiquity of the Spalding and Lancaster families on the American scene was not unrelated to the honored position won by a number of their members in the public life of pioneer Kentucky. And an important factor in accounting for the qualities of leadership they displayed was the ready response that they showed to the meager educational facilities afforded them in that primitive society.[3] The future bishop's mother was a case in point, for not only did she use her time to good advantage at the girls' academy taught by the Sisters of Loretto not many miles from Lebanon, a school where she received a training that was superior to that of most Kentucky women of her day, but she continued throughout her life to set a high store

3

upon the benefits of education. And it was from her that John Lancaster received his initial instruction and his introduction to the life of learning.

By the time that John was twelve he was ready for St. Mary's College, a boys' school near Lebanon founded in 1821 by Father William Byrne, a diocesan priest. The college had been recently returned to the diocesan clergy after a decade and a half of Jesuit control. John Lancaster entered the school — described by a contemporary as *"un petit séminaire* for such as might have a mission to the ecclesiastical state"[4] — in the autumn of 1852. That he profited from his five-year stay at St. Mary's was apparent at the end of the academic year 1856–1857 when he was awarded the first prize in religion, rhetoric, natural philosophy, chemistry, English composition, Latin, and French, along with high marks in music, algebra, and astronomy.[5]

There were few real colleges for Catholic boys in the United States in the 1850's, and no university properly so called. Among the best known institutions was Mount Saint Mary's College at Emmitsburg, Maryland, which was on the eve of its golden jubilee by the time that Spalding had finished his course at Lebanon. Mount Saint Mary's, under the direction of diocesan priests, was the second oldest Catholic boarding school for boys in the country, having opened in 1808. Late in the summer of 1857, then, the young Kentuckian made his way east, arriving at Emmitsburg on August 22. After

4

several months he wrote a letter to his mother that was revealing on several counts. He said:

> As to my education I think I might say that I am learning very fast. My mind is developing itself. And what before I saw confusedly are [sic] now becoming clear as the crystal light of day. I am studying hard. That is what I live on. Man's mental powers were not given to lie dormant and with God's grace if I have any, they shall be cultivated.[6]

It was the kind of letter that would gratify his first teacher, surely, to say nothing of the pride that she would feel in this premature display of judgment and reasoning quite beyond that of the ordinary youth of seventeen. Nor were they idle words, for Spalding's entire life bore witness to his love of intellectual pursuits, and the youthful pledge of cultivation of mind was more than fulfilled during the years ahead.

Beyond the fact that Spalding's ability in public address won him recognition as a speaker for St. John's Day, "one of the greatest collegiate festivals," as he told his mother, "since the sir [sic] name of both the Pres. [McCaffrey] and Vice-Pres. [McCloskey] is John,"[7] little more is known about his brief stay in Emmitsburg. Four days after the opening of the new McCaffrey Hall on January 11, 1858, a group of students were guilty of what the faculty judged a grave infraction of the rules, an incident which the historians of the institution describe only as "some disturbance . . . following an investigation into the contents of the boys' boxes, and several boys were expelled."[8] Precisely what the incriminating objects in the boxes were is not known, nor was the explanation offered by the chroniclers for this and other "rebellions" against faculty authority at the Mount in these years more enlightening than to attribute them to the lack of facilities for sports and the independent spirit prevalent among southern boys. Thus it was stated:

> Social conditions in the South particularly also account for a good deal of it, for the sons of planters were not accustomed to such severe discipline, and in fine, the spirit of independence was even more rampant than it is to-day amongst American youths, for they were nearer the Revolution.(!)[9]

In any case, Spalding was one of the culprits, and on January 18, he left Emmitsburg for Kentucky where his family allowed him to "cool his heels" until the opening of the new school year the following fall.

The next few months offer little by way of evidence for one interested in John Lancaster Spalding. One thing, however, is certain. By the time that he had attained his eighteenth birthday in that summer of 1858 his mind had been made up to study for the priesthood, and at that point in his life there was brought to bear upon all his future plans the strong influence of his uncle, Martin John Spalding, Bishop of Louisville. It was natural, of course, that both the parents and the young man himself should

6

defer to the bishop's superior knowledge and experience in these matters. The latter, like his nephew, had attended St. Mary's in Lebanon where he had been both student and teacher, and after further training at St. Thomas Seminary in Bardstown he had been sent to Rome for his theological studies at the Urban College of the Propaganda where he was ordained in 1834. In 1848 Martin Spalding was consecrated as coadjutor to Benedict Joseph Flaget, Bishop of Louisville, and upon the death of the venerable Sulpician prelate in 1850, he succeeded to the see. In true Spalding fashion, the bishop always showed the keenest interest in educational problems. It was due to his efforts, in large measure, and to those of Peter P. Lefevere, the Coadjutor Bishop and administrator of Detroit, that the American College at the Catholic University of Louvain was opened in March, 1857.

As Bishop of Louisville, Spalding's uncle was a suffragan of the Province of Cincinnati. He played a leading role in the first and second provincial councils convoked by the metropolitan in May, 1855, and May, 1858, being the author of the pastoral letters which were issued at the close of both councils. Closely associated with John B. Purcell, Archbishop of Cincinnati, who placed great confidence in him, Bishop Spalding had followed Cincinnati's educational developments at firsthand; consequently, he was well acquainted with Mount Saint Mary's of the West, the college and minor

7

seminary that had been opened by Purcell in September, 1856. It had been named after the Emmitsburg school where Purcell had spent over ten years of his life as student, professor, and president. In addition, most of its professors were graduates of the latter, and the course of studies and disciplinary regulations were modeled after those of the parent institution.[10] It was to Cincinnati, then, that young Spalding was sent in the fall of 1858, and it says something for his early reputation as a public speaker that, after only three weeks in residence, he should have been chosen as the students' spokesman at the simple ceremonies marking the school's second anniversary. During his academic year at Cincinnati, he showed the same proficiency that had marked his course in Lebanon. At the commencement on June 30, 1859, he was one of six young men who received the A.B. degree, and on that occasion he was valedictorian of the class with an oration on "The Spirit of English Literature," as well as the winner of the year's rhetorical honor. The president of Mount Saint Mary's of the West at the time was the convert priest, Sylvester H. Rosecrans, with whom Spalding was on friendly terms. That the relationship endured we know, for in 1877, when Spalding was making plans for his episcopal consecration, he invited Rosecrans, who had been named first Bishop of Columbus in 1868, to be the preacher.

Some years before John Lancaster took his degree

at Mount Saint Mary's of the West his uncle had begun arrangements for an American ecclesiastical college in Europe of which, as it turned out, the bishop's nephew became one of the early graduates. The idea grew out of the shortage of priests and teachers for the schools of the Diocese of Louisville, and when Bishop Martin Spalding went to Europe late in 1852 in search of personnel and found Englebert Cardinal Sterckx, Archbishop of Malines, favorably disposed to assist in the formation at Louvain of a college for the American missions, he was most enthusiastic. The elder Spalding fully appreciated the advantages offered by a house of studies in the immediate neighborhood of the Catholic University of Louvain, which had reopened in 1834, following an interval of almost forty years due to the turmoil of the French Revolution and its aftermath. The supply of priests was, indeed, his principal objective, but that did not cause him to lose sight of the need of a better educated clergy for the American Church. Following his visit with the Primate of Belgium in early January, 1853, he communicated the idea to Francis Patrick Kenrick, Archbishop of Baltimore, and among other things he said:

> Our studies in America are woefully below the European standard, and a few good missionaries educated in Belgium scattered through our various Dioceses would leaven the whole mass.[11]

After several false starts and initial setbacks the

plan finally gained enough support to warrant a beginning, and in March, 1857, the college was opened. It had been only a little over two years in operation, therefore, when Spalding finished at Cincinnati and was directed by his uncle to prepare to go abroad.

That Bishop Spalding assumed complete charge of his nephew's education we know from their correspondence. After the young man had been at Louvain for two months he informed his uncle of his general satisfaction with what he had found there. The bishop sent the letter on to Lancaster's father, remarking that it would probably not be as interesting to the family as it had been to him since, as he said, "he enters into details of his studies."[12] The intellectual side of the young man's training especially held the uncle's interest, as he made clear a week later when he wrote once more to his brother and outlined his plans for Richard Spalding's son. He said:

> I am truly rejoiced that he is so well satisfied, & that he is likely to do so well. Mr. Russell[13] writes me that he will be fully able to follow the higher courses because, besides a great aptitude for languages, he has quick & solid talent for the sciences. I am now more & more convinced that Louvain is the very place for him. The atmosphere & diet will develop his constitution, & make him strong & healthy, while the intellectual food will be the very thing he needs & is adapted for.
>
> When he will have finished at Louvain, it is my intention to send him for a year to Rome where, without

10

being under the rigid discipline of Colleges, he may be able to study the antiquities, & perfect himself in theology by attending the lectures. For this purpose, it will probably be necessary for him to be previously ordained at Louvain, so that he may be more free in his movements. God grant that he may persevere! In this event, I intend to spare no expense to bring him out, with all possible advantages, much greater even than I had.[14]

Persevere he did, benefiting all the while from the wise counsel of an episcopal uncle who thoroughly enjoyed the relationship and who eagerly seized upon every bit of news he could get about his promising nephew. As he told his brother in closing the lengthy letter quoted above, "Send me any letters you may receive from Lancaster."

On October 12, 1859, this young American arrived at Louvain, to begin what was to prove the most rewarding period of his student life. He was the first of five Kentucky Spaldings to study at the American College, and the last of the fifteen students to be enrolled for that particular school year. At that time the philosophy course lasted only one year, while three years were devoted to the study of theology, and Spalding spent an additional year attending courses at the university and preparing for the S.T.L. degree which he took on July 11, 1864.[15] From the fall of 1859, then — except for brief holidays — the American College was to be his home for approximately the next five years. If one were asked what was the strongest influence of the formative period of his life, it would doubtless be his stay at Louvain. As time passed, he grew to have a deep and abiding affection for the university as well as for his own college, and even the customary holidays at times found him content to stay close at hand by reason of his great liking for Belgium. As he told his parents on the eve of the summer vacation of 1862, "I can amuse myself better here than in another country, for the Belgians are the finest people in the world."[16] Spalding's love for his *alma mater* did not go unnoticed, and years later the historian of the institution remarked, "If ever an alumnus merited well of the College, it was he."[17]

Obviously, an American youth of nineteen from an obscure Kentucky village, entering a university for the first time, would take no active part in the controversies that preoccupied his elders during the early 1860's. Yet he would have been peculiarly insensitive to the currents of thought that swirled around him during his stay at Louvain, were he to have remained impervious to what he saw and heard and read. And Spalding was never one to be insensitive to intellectual stimulation. It happened that his time there coincided with a period when the remarkable leadership that Cardinal Sterckx had been giving to the Belgian Church since his advent to its primatial see in 1831 was still being vigorously exercised. Sterckx, more than any other

12

single man, was responsible for the reopening of the University of Louvain, closed since 1797, three years after he became primate. In the same year that he was named Archbishop of Malines a constitution was promulgated for the newly independent Kingdom of Belgium, and in it for the first time a traditionally Catholic people had, so to speak, come to terms with the liberal-democratic forces of the century in approving a separation of Church and State.

Thus there were certain Belgian constitutional provisions, such as the freedom guaranteed to private religious schools, that were familiar to young Spalding, although the grant of voluntary religious instruction for the public schools and government salaries for the clergy would be new to him. But there was a very real difference between the situation in Belgium and that in the United States as far as the spirit that animated governmental relations to religious matters was concerned. The germ of anticlericalism that had long flourished in western Europe had not passed Belgium by, and as a consequence a bitter struggle developed between the anti-clericals and the Catholics after some years. This is not the place to retell that story, but it is worthy of mention that the Belgian clergy and laity — superbly led by their cardinal primate to whom his fellow bishops were closely united — revealed around the mid-century a disciplined activity and

13

intelligent awareness concerning public issues affecting the Church that were largely lacking elsewhere in Europe.[18]

As a result, Lancaster Spalding was given a first-hand demonstration of how a people, predominantly Catholic and forced to grapple with a political regime hostile to their religious faith, reacted. With the inspiring leadership of Cardinal Sterckx they closed ranks and forged lawful instruments of resistance which, even though they were not always successful in preventing the realization of the opponents' objectives, at least gave the anti-clericals pause and showed that attempts to wrest from them fundamental rights, such as freedom of religious instruction, would not be achieved without a fight. It was an instrument of this kind that emerged at Malines four months before Spalding was ordained a priest when on August 18–23, 1863, the sessions of the first Catholic congress met with such success that they not only heartened the Belgians but also their beleaguered coreligionists of other lands.

Another aspect of Belgian life touched Spalding more closely. No university that is worthy of the name would expect, or desire, intellectual conformity to the degree of creating a complete absence of differences within its community of scholars. In this sense Louvain was a true intellectual center where the clash of ideas and the exchange of arguments not only advanced truth by refining the points at issue, but likewise served as a challenge

14

to both professors and students. Needless to say, there was nothing comparable to it that Spalding could have found in the American seminaries of that day or later. At the time of his arrival a controversy of this kind had been raging at Louvain for several years between Professor Casimir Ubaghs and his followers, whose journal, *La revue catholique,* expounded the principles of the ontologico-traditionalist school and the opposing party who attacked them in the *Journal historique et littéraire.* Through the first two years of Spalding's stay the ontologist quarrel continued until Ubaghs' theories were censured by a decree of the Holy Office in September, 1861, after which the controversy gradually died down.

Given his intellectual alertness, it would have been strange if an environment of this kind had not left an impression on Spalding. Yet to suggest that he was completely preoccupied with intellectual matters in these years would be false. Like the vast majority of seminarians he, too, was filled with a high idealism that prompted him to view most questions *sub specie aeternitatis.* For example, in the spring of 1861 he remarked to his uncle that while learning was, indeed, valuable in winning the respect of the world for the Catholic faith, it had converted very few souls. "Our religion is supernatural," he said, "and only those actions which proceed from supernatural motives are efficient for the good of religion."[19] That he was kept busy, there was no doubt, for in addition to following the courses in theology, Scripture, canon law, etc., at the university, he taught a class in English twice a week in the American College for students — mostly Belgians and Germans — who were preparing for the American missions.[20] Having brought to Europe what might be called a good student's knowledge of French, he now availed himself of the opportunity to learn German, a language in which he became proficient and to which in later life he gave more attention than he did to French.

After three years Spalding was awarded his first Louvain degree, the S.T.B., on July 7, 1862, and another year and a half brought him to the priesthood, which he received at the hands of Cardinal Sterckx on December 19, 1863. The remainder of that academic year was spent in finishing his work for the S.T.L. degree which he took on July 11, 1864. Earlier that year he had taken up with his uncle the question of the next step in his training, and in the spring he informed his father and mother of the outcome when he said:

> About a month ago I received also a letter from Uncle Martin in which he approved of the plan which I had suggested to him as to how I am to pass the coming scholastic year. I will leave Louvain about the middle of July for Germany where I will remain three or four months. Thence I will pass over into Italy and go down to Rome where I will stay until next summer.[21]

Except for a shorter stay in Germany than he had originally planned, this itinerary was followed

16

in the main. Immediately after receiving his degree, then, the young priest left Louvain and proceeded to Baden where, as he told his parents, the "principal reason" drawing him to that part of Germany was the University of Freiburg. Here he attended the lectures of several men with considerable reputations, such as Johann Baptist Alzog, the church historian, and Alban Isidor Stolz, a professor of theology. An additional reason why he sought this experience was, as he said, that the lectures were delivered in German, thus affording him an opportunity to perfect his knowledge of that language.[22] Spalding enjoyed his time in Germany, where he found much to admire in the kindness of the Freiburg professors and the warmth and hospitality of the priests; and he was likewise happy to report to his uncle that the German bishops had a good reputation for high moral and scientific standards.[23] July, 1864, found both uncle and nephew making major moves, for on the last day of that month Martin John Spalding took possession of the Archdiocese of Baltimore, having been promoted to the premier see to fill the vacancy caused by the death of Francis Patrick Kenrick. Archbishop Spalding intended that his nephew be incardinated into Baltimore as one of his priests. When he told John Lancaster of his desire, the latter expressed his willingness to do anything that he might wish. "I will never be able to repay you for all you have done for me," he said, "but I will try to do all that I can. Then I

17

leave it entirely to you as to whether I am to go to Baltimore or to Louisville."[24] As it turned out the long vacancy in the See of Louisville continued until September, 1865, when Peter J. Lavialle was consecrated a bishop. And since neither Lavialle nor his successor, William G. McCloskey, reacted favorably to the suggestion of excardinating Father Spalding for Baltimore, the latter never saw service as one of his uncle's priests.

Meanwhile Spalding had proceeded by slow stages to Rome where he arrived in early October, and by mid-November he was in a position to give his uncle a report on his new situation. Father Bernard Smith, O.S.B., professor of theology in the Urban College of Propaganda and friend of Archbishop Spalding and other American bishops, informed him that his uncle had written of his wish that he should concentrate on canon law. "Consequently," he said, "I have resolved to devote my time exclusively to that branch of sacred science." To that end he was reviewing privately what he had already seen of canon law, attending the lectures of two professors at the Sapienza, and he intended to assist at the discussions of the Congregation of the Council. That Rome had not superseded his loyalty to Louvain was evident when he remarked that he had already seen a good deal of canon law at the latter place "where it is undoubtedly better and more profoundly taught than here in Rome."[25]

Father Spalding likewise availed himself of the special opportunities that Rome offered, such as visiting the catacombs under the guidance of Dr. Smith and chatting with Dr. Augustin Theiner, the learned Prefect of the Vatican Archives, who had been one of his uncle's professors and whom he found editing a group of manuscripts. All of this John Lancaster described for Archbishop Spalding, together with an increasingly detailed commentary on European political and social trends. One of the things that prompted him to this sort of thing was the publication of Pius IX's encyclical *Quanta cura* with the attached *Syllabus of Errors* which, he said, had made "a good deal of noise" in Europe, where many felt that Montalembert's liberal principles now stood condemned. If the archbishop had heard that Louvain's philosophy had been condemned, it was untrue. Ubaghs would have to change some of his propositions because they were ambiguous and susceptible of a false meaning, but the real philosophical doctrines of Louvain, Spalding maintained, had not been condemned nor would they ever be. Acknowledging that a strong party in Belgium suspected the orthodoxy of some of the Louvain professors, Spalding was prompted to a spirited defense of intellectual freedom. He said:

There is nothing so sad as this prurient eagerness for finding heresy in every Catholic writer of talent and original thought who does not happen to think on every point as our own little selves. Besides being the

19

source of divisions and disputes among Catholics which it would be better to avoid especially in our age, this passion for heresy-finding often weakens the energy and deadens the efforts of the best and noblest writers, and champions of the Catholic cause.[26]

The young priest's lengthy digressions on the evils of popular government and the liberal philosophy, as well as on many other theoretical subjects, finally became tedious to the busy Archbishop of Baltimore who wished, indeed, to hear from him, but not in this vein. "Write me soon," he said early in 1865, "& tell me *facts & news;* do not write speculations."[27] Although John Lancaster's letters may thereafter have taken on a more sober tone, he did not altogether abandon expressing his personal reactions to current affairs. Thus, in reporting to his uncle that the stranded Bishop of Charleston, Patrick N. Lynch, was still in Rome, he was prompted to say that he believed the South was nearing exhaustion, and since that seemed to be the only way of ending the war, the sooner it came the better. "I certainly grieve over the miseries of our country," he said, "but I prefer anything to disunion." At that point recollection of the recent warning brought a pause, and he added, "But I stop here lest I should begin to speculate."[28]

By this time Father Spalding's European sojourn was coming to an end, and he announced that he would leave for home soon after Easter, and that, if nothing intervened, he should be in Baltimore

20

about the middle of May. It was a greatly chastened land to which he returned in that spring, with General Lee's surrender on April 9 and the capture a month later of Jefferson Davis symbolizing the prostration that had overtaken the South on the borders of which the Spalding interests were centered in Kentucky and Baltimore. During his first months in the United States he was given no definite assignment, a status that was not displeasing to Archbishop Spalding, since he had not abandoned hope of getting him for Baltimore where, as he said, he could employ him without delay. The nephew's uncommitted status in Louisville might possibly, he thought, "induce the new Bishop to give you to me." Regardless of the outcome, however, he was resigned to it. "We must leave this to the march of events," the archbishop added, "which God alone can dispose for the best."[29] In the sequel, as we have seen, Spalding remained a priest of the Diocese of Louisville.

At this point John Lancaster Spalding stood midway between the beginning of his formal education at St. Mary's in Lebanon and the event that was to shape the remainder of his life, namely, his call to the episcopacy. Twelve and a half years had passed since he began his schooling at St. Mary's, a period during which his uncle's hopes for him had been largely realized. Now he was at the threshold of a second twelve-year period that would witness the maturing of his intellectual powers and the flowering of his special talents for writing and preaching such as to win gradual recognition among his contemporaries that in this young priest the Catholic Church had a spokesman of singular originality, strength of mind, and gift of expression.

Yet Spalding's situation between 1865 and his episcopal consecration in 1877 was such that he could devote relatively little time to the intellectual work that held so strong an attraction for him. Besides his duties as an assistant at the Cathedral of the Assumption in Louisville, a busy downtown church even at that early date, he was made secretary to Bishop Lavialle soon after the latter's installation in the fall of 1865. He retained these positions during the first years of Lavialle's successor, William G. McCloskey. Thereafter he served briefly as chancellor of the diocese, as an editor of the *Catholic Advocate,* the diocesan weekly newspaper, and as pastor of St. Augustine's Church, the first parish in the city for Negro Catholics, which he founded in 1869. In addition to all these assignments — and this is more pertinent to our purpose — McCloskey put him in charge of the cathedral school taught by the Xaverian Brothers, of whom the bishop had become quite critical. He told Archbishop Purcell that the school was "nearly broken up" twice over the removal of a popular brother, adding, "it will require all the efforts of Father Spalding to bring it up again."[30]

Although the young priest was separated by many

22

miles from his uncle, they kept in close touch with each other. Knowing how forcefully John Lancaster later campaigned for a university for the American Church, one is tempted to see his influence behind his uncle, who was the first American bishop to record his desire for such an institution. By August, 1865, the Archbishop of Baltimore was actively engaged in preparations for another plenary council. In a letter of that summer dealing with conciliar business he posed the question for John Timon, Bishop of Buffalo: "Why should we not have a Catholic university?" And he then added, "It would be a great thing, if we could only agree as to the location & arrangement."[31] The archbishop's correspondence at this time reveals how eager he was to make a beginning, but it was equally obvious that he received little or no support from his fellow bishops. Consequently, when the subject arose at the council in October, 1866, the dire financial straits of the American College in Rome offered a plausible excuse for killing any action on a university, and nothing was done other than to express the desirability for such an institution. In this council, over which his uncle presided as apostolic delegate, Father Spalding's role was a minor one as one of three theologians to Francis Norbert Blanchet, Archbishop of Oregon City, and as the preacher on October 10 of one of the series of sermons in the cathedral.

But once the subject of a university had been

formally raised, it refused to die, and few were more anxious to keep it alive than the Spaldings. Disappointed as they were at the outcome in 1866, the uncle and nephew continued to follow closely whatever was said on the subject, and a year before the former's death the younger man contributed to the *Catholic Advocate* of January 28, 1871, a lengthy editorial that was about as cogent a presentation of the case for a Catholic university as had yet appeared anywhere in the United States. Calling attention to the fact that most of the writing done within the American Catholic community was by converts to the faith, he felt that a humiliating confession of this kind, when candidly admitted, might do some good. "There is in the church of this country," he remarked, "a deplorable dearth of intellectual men." Few young men of outstanding talent turned toward the priesthood, and if this condition persisted it would mean the perpetuation of a mediocre clergy. It was here that the lack of a university showed up, for there were no great seats of learning where the intellectual tastes of American Catholics could be fostered as was true of the universities in England, Germany, France, and Belgium, and, too, of Harvard and Yale in this country whence, as he said, "the rays of literary taste and culture have been diffused throughout the land." True, there were American Catholic schools that called themselves universities. "But these titles deceive no one," he maintained, "and provoke no comment, out of respect to the spirit of humbug which is prevalent with us."

It was likewise true that there were Catholic institutions available in Europe where American candidates for the priesthood could acquire a superior training. But this should never be permitted to obscure "the very great good which the Catholics of this country would derive from a university of their own." The freedom of action allowed in the United States, as well as the abundant means, removed any serious obstacles on that score, and Spalding felt confident that the Catholic laity would "eagerly engage in an enterprise, in which they have such great interests, both as Catholics and American citizens." Were a university to be established it would create a demand for talent, and by so doing talent would be called forth. Nor would he admit that local and personal prejudices were strong enough to stifle the realization of an enterprise which, he felt, was of "vital importance to the highest interests of the church in the United States." During the next decade he would frequently employ these same arguments as he continued to goad his coreligionists about the need for a university.

On February 7, 1872, John Lancaster Spalding lost his great patron and mentor when the seventh Archbishop of Baltimore was taken in death. Although the two were quite unlike in temperament, among the things that the uncle and nephew had in common was a love of learning for its own sake and a desire to create the best possible conditions wherein it might flourish. It so happened that the latter's first book was the biography of his uncle, and in that volume he not only gave generous treatment to the late archbishop's efforts for university education,[32] but he was at pains to portray his breadth of mind and deep appreciation for intellectual distinction. He described the great care with which Martin Spalding had assembled in Baltimore the best theological talent available for the plenary council of 1866, and in that connection he said:

> Nothing gave him greater delight than to place learning and genius in the service of religion. He had not the weakness to imagine that the Church is not capable of satisfying all the intellectual wants of even the most gifted minds; or that, because a man is able, he should be looked upon with distrust. If great minds have proved untrue to the Church, so have little minds. . . .[33]

Such, of course, was very much the spirit of the younger Spalding himself, free as he always was of that intellectual narrowness that at times overtakes certain churchmen and makes it difficult for them to appreciate an opposing point of view or to see the need on occasion to break with the traditional way of doing things in order to further the Church's welfare.

Meanwhile life under Bishop McCloskey had become increasingly unhappy for Spalding, due to differences about administrative policy and to the strained relations that had developed between the bishop and the Spalding family over certain projects that Martin had initiated during his days as Bishop of Louisville. Thus, when an opportunity to get away presented itself in the suggestion that he take over the writing of the life of Archbishop Spalding, whose personal papers had been deposited with Father Isaac Hecker, C.S.P., in New York, he eagerly seized it. He left Louisville in 1872 and for the next five years he was in residence first at the Paulist mother house on 59th Street and then at St. Michael's Rectory at 9th Avenue and 32nd Street, where he had the status of an assistant to the pastor, Father Arthur J. Donnelly. Spalding's special competence in educational matters was not long in coming to the fore in New York as it had in Louisville, and on September 26, 1874, the New York *Freeman's Journal* announced that he had been appointed director of the schools maintained by St. Michael's Parish. He also found time here for considerable writing — beyond the biography of his uncle — and in 1875 the Catholic Publication Society brought out two reading books that he had compiled and edited, which were followed two years later by a volume entitled *Essays and Reviews*.

By the time that Spalding had reached his mid-thirties he had already attracted considerable notice by his carefully prepared sermons and lectures and by his articles and books. While he had not, as has been said, played a conspicuous part in the plenary council of 1866, his presence there brought him

to the attention of a number of influential churchmen, and his prestige was further enhanced by the
biography of Archbishop Spalding, which revealed
not only a facile pen and a strong mind but, too, a
good grasp of the parochial problems of the Catholic Church in this country. It was not surprising,
therefore, when the new See of Peoria was erected
by Pope Pius IX on February 12, 1875 — and the
first candidate, Father Michael Hurley, pastor of
St. Patrick's Church in Peoria, declined the honor
— that those responsible for advising the Holy See
in these matters should have suggested to the Congregation de Propaganda Fide the name of John
Lancaster Spalding, a young, vigorous, and intellectually alert priest who seemed more than equal
to the burden of establishing a new diocese in his
native Middle West. Having lived for the previous
five years in his jurisdiction, Spalding chose as his
consecrator John Cardinal McCloskey, Archbishop
of New York, who performed the ceremony on
May 1, 1877, in old St. Patrick's Cathedral in Mott
Street with James Gibbons, Bishop of Richmond
and future cardinal, and Thomas Foley, Coadjutor
Bishop of Chicago, as co-consecrators.

Needless to say, it was no easy task for a young
and inexperienced bishop to organize a vast section
of north central Illinois, covering over 18,000
square miles with extremely limited Catholic re-
sources, into a viable unit of the Universal Church.[34]
At the time the Catholics in the area were estimated

at about 45,000, served by fifty-one priests in seventy-five churches and mission stations. Of these congregations, however, only twelve had parochial schools with a total enrollment of 2,010 students. That Spalding should have made the parochial school a special object of his zeal was to be expected of one who since his youth had attached such great importance to religious education. Although the statistics of the Church's directories of these years are not very trustworthy, they would seem to make it clear that the new bishop lost no time in putting his educational theories into practical operation, for in a single year six new parochial schools appeared in the diocese, to increase the number of children receiving their elementary education under Catholic auspices by almost 700 over the total that Spalding found on his arrival.[35] Moreover, this emphasis was maintained through the coming years, as can be seen from the fact that upon Spalding's resignation in 1908 the reported Catholic population of 123,500 for the diocese was almost thrice the 45,000 mentioned for 1878, whereas the rate of increase in schools was almost double that in population, with the eighteen schools of 1878 having by 1908 reached seventy with a combined enrollment of 11,360 students.[36] Meanwhile the bishop also gave support to secondary education by his encouragement of the academies for girls conducted by various religious congregations of women, and by his initiative in opening in 1899 a diocesan high school for boys, Spalding Institute, which was placed in charge of the Brothers of Mary.

In fairness to Bishop Spalding's memory the above facts relating to education in the Diocese of Peoria in his time should be kept in mind, since there were not lacking critics who maintained that as he became more deeply involved in national questions his diocesan responsibilities suffered in consequence. Whatever aspects of diocesan life may have been overlooked, it would be difficult to prove that education had been neglected during his tenure of the See of Peoria. That the succeeding years witnessed an increasing involvement on Spalding's part in extradiocesan activities is altogether true; yet none of this was alien to or inappropriate for an American bishop. For example, in the early 1880's he expended a tremendous amount of time and energy in behalf of the Irish Catholic Colonization Association of which he had been elected president in May, 1879.[37] Strictly speaking, this was not the type of thing that one normally associates with education; yet it has a place here in that Spalding influenced the action of a number of Irish immigrant families and enlightened thousands of others concerning the superior advantages to be found on the farms of the West over the stifling existence that many of them were then leading in the industrial slums of the eastern cities.

With that objective in mind in June, 1879, Spalding undertook, in the company of John Ireland, Bishop of St. Paul, an extended and exhausting lecture tour during which they spoke to large audiences in Boston, New York, Philadelphia, Baltimore, and other cities. The immigrants were encouraged to relocate in the West, while Catholics of means were urged to purchase stock certificates in the company that Spalding and his associates were then organizing. As a further means of attaining their goal, Spalding that year wrote his third book, *The Religious Mission of the Irish People and Catholic Colonization,* which a recent historian has described as "certainly the most distinguished piece of scholarly writing produced by the colonization movement. . . ."[38] Characterizing the Irish at the outset as "the most important element" in the American Church,[39] Spalding conceived their role to be to spread the Catholic faith throughout the United States. That was why he was so eager that they should move to the West, for his five-year residence in lower Manhattan Island had left him with an unshakeable conviction that the principal cause of leakage from the Church was what he called "the fatal and never sufficiently to be deplored concentration of the Irish immigrants in the great cities, the factory towns, and the mining districts."[40] In comparison to this he considered all other causes to be insignificant. If in the end his labors, and those of his associates in the I.C.C.A., failed to bring about the relocation of the immigrant Irish in large numbers on the western farmlands, the

31

fault was not theirs. At least Spalding had put before them in his lectures and in his book a plan for a more wholesome life, which many of them ignored to their personal detriment as well as to the loss of the Catholic Church in this country.

At the same time that Bishop Spalding was devoting attention to the Irish Catholic Colonization Association he was quickening the pace of his campaign for the institution about which he and his uncle had begun to dream nearly twenty years before. As it happened, the panic of 1873 resulted in conditions that seemed to open up a new opportunity for the start of a Catholic university. The shaky economic conditions that persisted long after the first shock that accompanied the failure of the Jay Cooke banking house in September, 1873, were felt nowhere in Catholic circles with more force than in the Archdiocese of Cincinnati.[41] Late in 1878 disaster overtook the private banking business of Father Edward Purcell, brother of John B. Purcell, the aged Archbishop of Cincinnati, and among the losses that ensued was Mount Saint Mary's Seminary of the West, which had to be closed for nearly a decade. Knowing the desperate plight of Archbishop Purcell and his coadjutor, William Henry Elder, Spalding approached the latter in the summer of 1880 with an inquiry as to how he would look upon the American bishops taking over the Cincinnati seminary and converting it into a national school for advanced theology, or, as he phrased it, "a beginning towards founding a Catholic university. . . ." He told Elder:

> I see no other way by which we can hope to raise the standard of Clerical Education and you know better than I how difficult it is to find priests who have the learning which bishops ought to have; and as our dioceses are becoming so numerous it seems to me to be necessary to set about doing something in earnest by which we may raise up a class of men in the priesthood who will become the ornament and the strength of our holy faith.[42]

Elder took readily to the proposal, and for several months the two prelates continued their exchange of views. But they both realized that nothing of a really binding character could be done without the authority and backing of the leading members of the episcopal body. And for that reason their hopes received a severe jolt when Spalding's appeal to the titular head of the hierarchy, Cardinal McCloskey, met with a veto of their plan.

For many men that would have been the end of the story. But among the admirable qualities of the Bishop of Peoria was the kind of courage that refused to permit a good idea to be buried beneath a series of disappointments. Thus, when he was invited to deliver the sermon at the silver jubilee Mass of St. Francis Seminary in Milwaukee on June 30, 1881, he determined upon another major effort to enlist support for his idea. He first reviewed in brief the fame that had redounded to the Church from the learning and eloquence of its outstanding

33

priests. Contributions such as those made by these men, he said, rested upon the best possible intellectual training, and here he called the roll of great churchmen like St. Charles Borromeo, Reginald Cardinal Pole, St. Francis de Sales, St. Vincent de Paul, Father Jacques Olier, and the sons of St. Ignatius Loyola at their society's Roman colleges who had made such remarkable contributions to the education of the Catholic clergy. Spalding was at pains to express admiration for the work then being done by the seminaries of the American Church, and he trusted, therefore, that he would not be misunderstood if he affirmed that it was not possible that seminaries "such as these are and must remain, here and elsewhere, should give the highest intellectual education."[43] They were no more than elementary seminaries, and among them he would include the American colleges at Louvain and Rome.

What was needed was something beyond the purely professional training to which the ordinary seminary was limited by its nature. Here the bishop proceeded to outline what he had in mind, and it is odd to find him saying that he did not intend a university but, as he remarked, "something far simpler, less expensive, and, in my opinion, better fitted to supply the most pressing want of American Catholics. The institution of which I am thinking," he said, "might be called a High School of Philosophy and Theology."[44] The experience of the last few years had obviously chastened Spalding and dictated a more modest approach to the problem, one that would more readily gain support. But if his goal had been modified since he first raised the question, his insistence that something be undertaken had grown stronger. To those who told him that it was inopportune and that an institution such as he had in mind was not possible, he replied, "I make answer that it is possible to try. . . . Ambitious men may fear failure, but good men need not be subject to this weakness."[45]

Any project as ambitious as that which Bishop Spalding was then trying to forward will inevitably encounter opposition. Yet often ground is gained in that very way by having the opposition state its case and by clarifying the issue in public debate. And that is what occurred after the Milwaukee sermon. Early in 1882 a new volume of the Bishop of Peoria appeared containing the text of the sermon along with other essays.[46] He sent a copy of the book to some of the leading bishops, and from among them James Gibbons, Archbishop of Baltimore, wrote to commend him for his literary efforts. To have on one's side the occupant of the premier see, especially when he was a prelate of such wide influence as Gibbons, would be a distinct advantage. For that reason Spalding did not let the matter drop there; he thanked the archbishop for his kind

words, remarked how difficult it was for a mission-
ary bishop to write anything worthwhile in the midst
of his numerous interruptions, and he then stated:

> If we could only begin a university college for the
> higher education of priests, it would be my greatest
> happiness to go into it and devote the rest of my life
> to this work, which, I am convinced, is of all others the
> most important and the most urgent.[47]

This was the ultimate that any man could pledge
to a cause, and the earnestness of the offer must
have made an impression on Gibbons. Discussion
of the question grew as time went on with journals
like the *American Catholic Quarterly Review* and
Catholic newspapers like the *Freeman's Journal* of
New York having much to say pro and con a university for the Catholics of the country, while
simultaneously it became a subject for increased
comment in the private correspondence of the
bishops.[48]

Despite adverse criticism the determination of the
Bishop of Peoria remained fixed, and when it came
time for him to make his first *ad limina* visit to
Rome to report on his diocese, he decided to carry
the matter to a higher level. Father Patrick Hennessy, pastor of St. Patrick's Church in Jersey City,
for example, told Bernard J. McQuaid, Bishop of
Rochester, late in 1882, "Bishop Spalding told me
the other day that he intended to bring the subject
of the High School of Theology to the notice of the
Holy Father."[49] It was natural that Spalding should

make this appeal since his attempts with individual American bishops had met with no real success, and he knew that in any case ultimate authorization for a university would have to come from the Holy See. Hostile to Spalding's idea from the outset, McQuaid kept as close watch on the moves of his brother bishop as possible, and he was cheered by rumors that the latter's "pet work," as he called it, had fallen through. Actually, McQuaid was on sounder ground when he informed Bishop Richard Gilmour of Cleveland, "Now they say he is working for a national council."[50] Spalding was not the only bishop from the Middle West who was working for a plenary council at this time, and in the end the opposition of the eastern bishops was overridden and Rome gave orders that the American hierarchy should prepare for another plenary gathering.

Preoccupation with plans for a Catholic university in the United States did not cause Spalding to forget his *alma mater*. When Father John De Nève, Rector of the American College, Louvain, sent out a letter and circular to the alumni in January, 1882, they met with a warm response from the Bishop of Peoria. He was delighted that De Nève was again in the rector's chair after an interval of ten years, since he had not approved of his predecessor's regime, and he was pleased, too, to learn of De Nève's plans for the celebration of the silver jubilee of the college on March 19. But what caught his eye in particular in the rector's report was an item relating to superior students attending courses at the University of Louvain. Never neglecting a chance to improve the education of the clergy, he said:

> I am especially glad to see from your letter that the better sort of students will be permitted to follow the university course. This is undoubtedly very important, and was, as you know, a chief reason for founding the College at Louvain.[51]

To return to the proposed council of the American bishops. The holding of a plenary assembly had been rendered certain in May, 1883, when the Cardinal Prefect of Propaganda addressed a letter to the metropolitans of the United States informing them of Leo XIII's wish that they should come to Rome the following November to plan the agenda for such a gathering. There was no progress in the university question at the Roman conferences, where it was not even mentioned, but in the meantime Spalding had succeeded in giving the whole idea an air of genuine reality when he secured the promise of Miss Mary Gwendolen Caldwell, a young heiress of a family known to the Spaldings in Kentucky, to give $300,000 toward starting such an institution. Two weeks before the opening of the council, therefore, he wrote to Archbishop Gibbons to request seats for Miss Caldwell and her party, who would be present in the cathedral for the formal opening, and he remarked that since the discourse on higher education that he was to give was quite lengthy it might be well to assign him an evening rather than to schedule it for one of the morning Masses. Gibbons was quite agreeable to the suggestion, and thus the evening of November 16 was set aside for Spalding's sermon on "The Higher Education of the Priesthood," which the Baltimore *Sun* of the following day noted as his "favorite theme" upon which, they said, he had preached a sermon that was regarded as "a powerful one." Spalding first dwelt upon the services rendered to the Church by its highly trained clergy, and spoke of how much intellectual training had done for the churchmen themselves. It had freed them, he said, from the common error of placing undue importance on their own thinking in view of the knowledge they had acquired of the best thoughts that live in the world's great literature. Tracing in broad strokes the main intellectual currents to the western world since the Middle Ages, he mentioned the nineteenth century's advance in science and the loss of supernatural faith that had accompanied it on the part of many. The continuance and progress of doubt and religious indifference were, he maintained, to be ascribed in part to the fact that for over a century earnest believers in God and Christianity had been, as he expressed it, "less eager to acquire the best philosophic and literary cultivation of mind than others who, having lost faith in the supernatural, seek for compensation in a wider and deeper knowledge of nature. . . ."[52]

Bishop Spalding then returned to an aspect of the subject that was a familiar refrain with him, namely, the narrowness of purely professional training. If priests were to escape this defect, he said, they must be given a chance for study at an institution of greater breadth and depth than an ecclesiastical seminary whose curriculum and methods made it "simply a training college for the practical work of the ministry." Repeating his tribute of three years before at Milwaukee to the good work done by the American seminaries, he nevertheless insisted:

The ecclesiastical seminary is not a school of intellectual culture, either here in America or elsewhere, and to imagine that it can become the instrument of intellectual culture is to cherish a delusion. . . . Its methods are not such as one would choose who desires to open the mind, to give it breadth, flexibility, strength, refinement, and grace. Its textbooks are written often in a barbarous style, the subjects are discussed in a dry and mechanical way, and the professor, wholly intent upon giving instruction, is frequently indifferent as to the manner in which it is imparted; or else not possessing himself a really cultivated intellect, he holds in slight esteem expansion and refinement of mind, looking upon it as at the best a mere ornament. I am not offering a criticism upon the ecclesiastical seminary, but am simply pointing to the plain fact that it is not a school of intellectual culture, and consequently, if its course were lengthened to five, to six, to eight, to ten years, its students would go forth to their work with a more thorough professional training, but not with more really cultivated minds.[53]

Seminaries, then, could not give the type of training that was necessary; only a university could do that, and so long as American Catholics looked to what Spalding called "the multiplying of schools and seminaries [rather] than to the creation of a real university," their progress would be slow and uncertain.

To the Bishop of Peoria there was no place more inviting for a university under the auspices of the Catholic Church than the United States where, he said, "almost for the first time in her history, the Church is really free." Without a university it was idle to speak of Catholics exercising a "determining force" in the controversies of the age. Catholics of wealth would go on sending their sons to universities where their religious faith would be endangered, and problems like necessary reforms in public life and defense of the rights of Catholics as citizens would in consequence fail to benefit from the wisdom and counsel that skillful Catholic leaders would inspire. The bishop was aware of the difficulties involved and the obstacles to be overcome, but he believed that if a beginning were made on a modest scale as, for example, with courses in theology and philosophy as had been true at Paris in the twelfth century and at Louvain at its reopening in 1834, it could be done. These subjects could form what he termed the "central faculty of a complete educational program," and around this nucleus other faculties would in time take their place and thus, as he put it, "the beginning which we make will grow, until like the seed planted in the earth, it shall wear the bloomy crown of its own development."

During the month-long sessions in Baltimore the Bishop of Peoria lost no opportunity to further his plan. His efforts were finally rewarded when the council voted to appoint a committee to handle the problem of a university. When Spalding came to summarize the council's work in the closing sermon in the Cathedral of the Assumption on Sunday, December 7, therefore, it was understandable that he should have proudly announced that the foundation of an institution had been laid that was destined, he said, to grow into a university, "the measure of whose usefulness, the grandeur of whose scope, and the fruitful blessings of which cannot be forecast by the mind."[54] It was a flight of oratory, but it was warranted under the circumstances. Once the idea had been formally approved by the hierarchy, the committee appointed to see to its realization was kept very busy with the developing details. And during the next five years no member of the committee was more active than Spalding in attending meetings, offering suggestions, counseling with various experts, begging for funds, etc. Thus it was fitting that he should have been chosen to deliver the address at the laying of the cornerstone of the original building on May 24, 1888, when President Grover Cleveland, several members of his cabinet, about thirty bishops, and a large gathering of clergy and laity were in attendance.

After reviewing the progress of the Church in the United States, the speaker launched into a tribute to the American form of government that had made it possible for Catholicism to have prospered without let or hindrance, and he emphasized that this progress had been made in a country where there was no union of Church and State. At the time of the founding of the American Republic, Spalding remarked, such an experiment had not yet been made, and the success that had attended the system for nearly a century was, he maintained, "of worldwide import, because this is the modern tendency and the position towards the Church which all the nations will sooner or later assume." In the same way all countries would ultimately be forced, he thought, to accept popular rule and what he called the "great underlying principle of democracy — that men are brothers and have equal rights, and that God clothes the soul with freedom," a truth taught by Christ and proclaimed by the Church.[55] Doubtless it was gratifying to Cleveland, his cabinet colleagues, and the audience in general to hear a Catholic bishop speak in this manner. But it was a far cry from the highly censorious ideas on popular government that he had expressed a quarter century before to his uncle while he was still in Europe. The interval of residence in the United

States and further reflection on European political developments had apparently caused him to change his mind on this question as he did on a number of other matters.[56]

Noting the American people's respect for law, the bishop stated that the United States had demonstrated that Church and State, although moving in separate orbits, could still co-operate for the common welfare. Mention was made of the advances of science which, Spalding said, were welcome to those Catholics who had the kind of confidence in the future that left no place for regrets about past ages such as those entertained by some of their coreligionists. He continued:

> The scientific habit of mind is not favorable to child-like and unreasoning faith, and the new views of the physical universe which the modern mind is forced to take, bring us face to face with new problems in religion and morals, in politics and society.

Here the university would render a great service by providing a hospitable atmosphere for both ancient wisdom and new learning, and that by teaching the best that was known as well as encouraging research into the unknown. After a defense of the position of religion in education as necessary for the completeness of mental discipline, the speaker closed by a graceful compliment to the university's principal donor, Miss Caldwell, "whose generous heart and enlightened mind," said Spalding, "were the impulse which has given to what had long been hope deferred and a dreamlike vision, existence and a dwelling place. . . ."[57]

The address was well received in the American press, both secular and Catholic. Obviously, however, someone had not been happy about Spalding's liberal and open-minded approach, for he was reported in an unfavorable light to the Congregation de Propaganda Fide at Rome. Nearly a year later Cardinal Simeoni, Prefect of Propaganda, wrote to inquire of Michael A. Corrigan, Archbishop of New York, about the Spalding speech which, he said, had been described as containing "strange ideas that were not too sound." Simeoni understood that copies were still available and, if this be so, he would like to have one; meantime the archbishop would please keep "this delicate affair" confidential.[58] Although nothing more was heard at the time about the speech of May, 1888, it made its contribution to the growing reputation of the Bishop of Peoria at the Roman Curia for being a man of 'liberal' views, and for that reason suspect in the eyes of some.

It is little wonder that John Lancaster Spalding should have attracted opposition, for on occasion the original cast of his thought and the fearless manner in which he expressed it startled conservative minds. There are few things that are more upsetting to many men than to criticize the traditional way in which they have been doing things and to introduce a sharp break with the past. For example, in Catholic circles at that time it was

45

customary to laud the Middle Ages and nostalgically to view that distant period as the 'age of faith.' It was a view that Spalding never shared. He was proud of being a man of his own century, and he saw nothing to be gained by investing the Middle Ages with a value that, in so far as he knew, in reality they had never possessed. Nor was he in the least disconcerted, as were many of his coreligionists, by the advances of modern science; on the contrary, he welcomed them and maintained that if properly understood they could be made to serve man's best interests without doing damage to his religious faith.

In this sense Spalding was an innovator. Yet he could console himself that St. Thomas Aquinas was also regarded as a dangerous innovator at the University of Paris in the 1260's by the secular priests, Gerard of Abbeville and Nicholas of Lisieux, whose low esteem for mendicant friars prompted their scorn of them as teachers; or more importantly, when the tenacity with which Siger of Brabant and his associates clung to the Aristotelianism of Averroes found a source of scandal in Aquinas' bold adventure in rearing up a Christian Aristotelianism of his own and provided the cause of another historic conflict within the university.[59] Spalding knew enough history, needless to say, to realize that this sort of thing was a more or less constant occurrence in the Church, and that any man who challenged the established order and tried to bring about reform must anticipate conflict. But it never occurred to him to yield ground in the face of the opponents. Furthermore, he was devoid of that type of ambition that prompts certain men to surrender their inner convictions lest they incur the displeasure of those who might have a deciding voice about their future. That is why, too, Spalding felt an instinctive sympathy for one whose fidelity to principle was at the root of his misfortune, as happened within the next few years to two men for whom he entertained a high regard, Bishop John J. Keane, Rector of the Catholic University of America, who was dismissed from his post in September, 1896, for his alleged 'liberalism' and Spalding's classmate, Monsignor Jean B. Abbeloos, who two years later was forced out of office as Rector of the Catholic University of Louvain over what the Bishop of Peoria described as "intrigues, originating in the University and fostered at Rome. . . ."[60]

Despite criticism of his ideas, however, Spalding continued to serve the cause in every way he could as, for example, by composing the national appeal for funds for the university that was issued to the Catholics of the United States in the name of the executive committee.[61] But oddly enough, when it came time in May, 1886, for the committee to choose a rector, Spalding declined the offer made to him by the so-called Atlantic archbishops — Gibbons, Corrigan, Patrick Ryan of Philadelphia, and

John Williams of Boston — who were empowered to make the choice. The man selected in his place was the Bishop of Richmond, John J. Keane, who in a memoir on his relationship to the university told about how Gibbons had informed him that Spalding had refused the rectorship "most positively," and had agreed with the archbishops that it should be Keane. "This Bishop Spalding himself repeated to me," said Keane, "adding that, for years to come, the post would practically be that of the President of a Seminary, a post which he could in no way be induced to fill."[62]

This is one of the most puzzling episodes in the life of John Lancaster Spalding. As previously mentioned, in July, 1882, he had told the Archbishop of Baltimore that if a university could be started it would be his "greatest happiness to go into it and devote the rest of my life to this work. . . ."[63] Yet less than four years later, when the chance presented itself for him to head the institution that he, more than any other single man, had done most to bring into being, he refused. Nor is the explanation of his action that he gave to Keane a satisfactory one, for Spalding knew perfectly well — as he had publicly stated more than once — that for some years the university would be hardly more than an advanced seminary.

In any case, Bishop Spalding did not slacken his support, and during the university's early years John J. Keane and his associates found in him a devoted friend and faithful collaborator. That the Catholic University of America remains, therefore, and always will remain, the greatest single monument to Spalding's zeal for education, is beyond question. Doubtless something of that kind was in the minds of Gibbons, Corrigan, Ryan, and Williams when they offered him the rectorship in May, 1886, as it remained in the minds of all who knew the true story of the institution's early history. It was the subject of public commendation in May, 1902, on the occasion of Spalding's silver jubilee as a bishop, and when eleven years later he reached the golden jubilee of his priesthood it was affirmed in ringing tones by the university's fourth rector, Thomas J. Shahan, who traveled to Peoria to pay tribute to the aged prelate where he reviewed the university's present prosperous state and then stated:

No one who knows the beginnings of this work will gainsay me when I say that all this is owing to John Lancaster Spalding, that it originated in his heart and mind, and that its first measure of realization was owing to his faith in such an enterprise, his readiness to lead with voice and deed, his power of inspiring the first generous and noble gift that made it possible to pass from velleities to action, and his wisdom and courage in its earliest years, when the new institution that he had called into being walked, so to speak, through the Valley of Dispute, and by the very old law of survival earned its right to go about the business for which it had been created by Leo XIII and the Catholic bishops of the United States.[64]

Finally, two years later, when the university

49

reached its own silver jubilee, James Gibbons, the cardinal chancellor, stated at a special Mass in St. Patrick's Church in Washington:

> All great works have their inception in the brain of some great thinker. God gave such a brain, such a man, in Bishop Spalding. With his wonderful intuitionary power, he took in all the meaning of the present and the future of the Church in America. If the Catholic University is today an accomplished fact, we are indebted for its existence in our generation, in no small measure, to the persuasive eloquence and convincing arguments of the Bishop of Peoria.[65]

The Catholic University of America will, indeed, always remain the principal monument to Spalding's memory as an educator. He was one of those fortunate men who not only conceive and dream about a great idea, but who witness its realization, and that in an institution that continues to serve into the indefinite future the cause they have sponsored. Nor was that all. Both by the spoken and written word, employed over a period of forty years, John Lancaster Spalding earned the distinction of having made the most significant contribution to education of any single member of the American Catholic community, as well as having won an honored place in the general educational picture of the United States of his time. From his early days as a priest in this country his unsigned articles in the *Catholic Advocate* of Louisville helped to shape the minds of his Kentucky coreligionists about educational problems, and once he had completed the biography of his uncle in New York, the remaining time that he lived there found him a regular contributor to the *Catholic World*. Thus a steady stream of articles, lectures, and sermons gradually impressed Spalding's name upon the public mind, and at intervals these lectures and articles were gathered up into more lasting form and published as books, as was the case, for example, in 1877, the year of his episcopal consecration, when his second volume appeared.[66]

Spalding was by no means consistent in all his educational ideas, but there was one view from which he rarely ever varied, namely, that the State should be kept at as great a distance as possible from the schools. And as a sort of corollary to this idea he exhorted the Catholics to shoulder the burden of supporting their own schools and not look to the State for financial aid. Needless to say, the problem was not nearly as complex in the late nineteenth century as it came to be at a later day when the full effects, as it were, of the practically mandatory legislation on parochial schools of the plenary council of 1884 had given rise to a vast educational system under Catholic auspices. Nor was there then any such issue as financial aid for the schools from the federal government, since the latter gave assistance to no schools except those maintained on the Indian reservations. Thus in the last quarter of the century sharp differences over school policies arose among the Catholics, and the views of the Bishop of Peoria were not shared by a considerable number of his coreligionists. In any case, the first of the two ideas mentioned above appeared early in his career when an essay he wrote commemorating the centennial of American independence took the form of summarizing the Catholic contribution to the history of this country. Noting the importance that Catholics attached to individual rights, he said:

> We believe that the man is more than the citizen; that when the state tramples upon the divine liberty of the wretched beggar, the consciences of all are violated; that it is its duty to govern as little as possible. . . . For this reason we believe that when the state assumed the right to control education, it took the first step away from the true American and Christian theory of government back towards the old pagan doctrine of state-absolutism.[67]

He may well have had in mind here President Grant's proposal of the previous year that no public funds should ever be allotted to religious education, a suggestion that set off a lively controversy and led to the framing of an amendment to the Constitution, sponsored by James G. Blaine, embodying Grant's idea. True, the so-called Blaine Amendment failed to pass Congress, but before the issue had ceased to occupy public attention angry words had been exchanged all over the land between the promoters of secular education and the sponsors of private religious schools.[68]

Yet the quarrel that broke over the schools in 1875 was not nearly so damaging to national unity

52

as the prolonged and bitter school controversies that occurred during the early 1890's. The excitement at that time — fanned by the American Protective Association's campaign against the Catholic Church — embraced virtually all classes of the population and, needless to say, no Catholic followed the debates over the relationship between the public and private religious schools more closely than the Bishop of Peoria. At the outset of the quarrel he deplored the sectarian and partisan tone that dominated so much of the talk on both sides, and in an effort to lift the discussion to a more profitable plane he counseled both Catholics and Protestants that they would be acting in a wiser and more helpful way if they would let this irritating issue — about which there was nothing new to be said — die. Rather than to go on with the argument they would be better advised, he thought, to "set themselves resolutely to work to improve educational methods." The school question, he maintained, would be settled by facts, not arguments, and thus for Catholics to insist on their grievances was only diverting them from their true goal, which was the education of their children. And as for those who accused them of sinister designs against the public schools, to Spalding they were either "bigots or politicians, and need not be taken seriously."[69] On the whole it was salutary advice, even if it fell largely on deaf ears and effected no noticeable diminution of the public clamor.

In fact, the years immediately ahead witnessed the perennial 'school question' draw more fire than ever before. The long and complicated story cannot be retold here, but two phases of it will illustrate how Spalding made his voice heard in the discussions about the educational problems with which Americans were grappling at that time. The first was confined to the bishop's own State of Illinois where in 1889 the legislature had enacted the Edwards Law, named for Richard Edwards, the Superintendent of Public Instruction, and intended to insure that every child would receive at least a minimum of education. According to this measure, every person having under his or her control a child between seven and fourteen years of age was compelled to see to it that the child attended a public school for at least sixteen weeks of each year under penalty of paying a fine of twenty dollars that would be turned over to the use of the public schools of the district. As a sort of afterthought, it was stated that if the child's parents or guardians could show that their charge had attended school for the required length of time in a private school approved by the board of education of the district, they would be free of any penalty. In other words, the burden of proof was put on the private school to demonstrate that it was an institution fit to perform the functions for which it was intended, and the judge of its fitness was to be the local public school board. Finally, in both the public and private schools the teaching of reading, writing, arithmetic, geography, and the history of the United States was to be conducted in the English language.[70]

Supported by both political parties, the Edwards Law passed the legislature almost unanimously and for a time encountered no opposition from any outside source. But after a similar measure of the same year in Wisconsin, the Bennett Law, became a storm center among Wisconsin's numerous German citizens — both Catholic and Lutheran — the Edwards Law was brought under closer scrutiny in Illinois. In both states those of German birth or extraction resented the barring of the German language in their private religious schools for the teaching of most of the subjects in the curriculum, and from this grievance the attack gradually broadened to other features of the Edwards and Bennett Laws. Matters were made much worse, of course, when the most influential newspaper in the region, Joseph Medill's Chicago *Tribune,* launched a sharp editorial campaign against the Catholics in both states. The already exasperated feelings engendered by the A.P.A., which was especially strong in Illinois, were further aggravated by the *Tribune's* editorial policy which was frequently expressed in terms such as these:

In Illinois and Wisconsin a contest between the supporters and enemies of the American free schools, between the right of Americans to make their own laws and the claim of an Italian priest living in Rome that he has the power to nullify them, can have but one termination — the defeat of such arrogance and presumption.[71]

Given provocation of this kind it was scarcely surprising that sentiment among Illinois' nearly three quarters of a million Catholics should have crystallized behind their bishops, who regarded it as an obligation in conscience not only to defend the Church against false charges, but likewise to affirm their support of the more than 270 parochial schools in which over 65,000 Catholic children were then enrolled in the four dioceses of the state.

Some weeks before the Illinois bishops decided upon taking joint action in the controversy Spalding had published an article with a view to explaining the nature of the Catholic educational exhibit at the World's Columbian Exposition in Chicago, of which he had been given charge by the hierarchy. In the face of the current criticism he in no way modified his customary insistence on the need for religious education. The Church, he said, would never consent to the exclusion of religion from any educational process, and since the public school system had finally become "exclusively secular," Catholics had no alternative but to build and maintain their own schools in which, as he expressed it, "the will, the head, and the conscience, as well as the intellect, should be educated."[72] The Church's exhibit at the Chicago exposition would demonstrate what American Catholics were doing to develop the kind of civilization in this country which, according to Spalding, was "in great part the outgrowth of religious principles, and which depends for its continued existence upon the morality which religious faith alone can make strong and enduring."[73]

Meanwhile the bishops of the ecclesiastical Province of Chicago had taken counsel with each other over the issues raised by the Edwards Law and had decided upon a joint pastoral letter as the best means of clarifying the Church's position for their priests and people. It was also as an outgrowth of this same controversy that they determined to establish a weekly Catholic newspaper as a medium through which their people might be kept informed of developments in this and other matters touching the Church. In this way the *New World* of Chicago had its beginning, and in its first issue of September 10, 1892, there was carried the pastoral letter of the Archbishop of Chicago, Patrick A. Feehan, and his three suffragans, the Bishops of Peoria, Alton, and Belleville.

Whether or not Bishop Spalding wrote the pastoral letter on education, it is impossible to say, although it read like him and it would be natural that he should have been chosen as the author since he knew much more about the subject than the other three prelates. In any case, the letter opened with a summary of the philosophy that lay behind the Church's insistence on religious education, after which readers were reminded of the legislation of

57

the plenary council of 1884 on parochial schools, as well as of the contributions that Catholics were making to the nation's welfare through their numerous religious schools. The bishops protested against the injustice of making Catholics contribute to the support of both public and parochial schools, but they acknowledged that for the present there seemed to be no escape from the double burden. And they would not have Catholics seek excuses in such things as these for not complying with their duty to support the parochial schools. "To prefer life to honor is justly held to be base," they said, "and where there is question of fidelity to truth and principle, financial and economical considerations are out of place." As for the Edwards Law, it was characterized as "an insidious and unjust" measure which violated the rights of Catholics as citizens. The bishops then stated:

> Freedom of worship implies and involves freedom of education. If the State may dictate to us what kind of school we shall have, it may make it a penal offense not to frequent the church it may select. We denounce this law as a violation of our constitutional rights, and hold that those who favor it are unworthy of the support of an enlightened and fair minded voter. Let us use all right and honorable means to have it repealed, and let the designing and bigoted be taught that the WEST is not a field in which their labors will bear fruit.[74]

As was to be expected, the Illinois press was for the most part unfriendly to the Catholics in the

58

controversy, a type of reaction that Spalding met in the leading paper of his see city, the Peoria *Journal.* In its issue of October 19 the *Journal* had an editorial entitled "Secret Societies" which was critical of the Church as the enemy of the public schools, and the same issue carried a letter from a certain E. E. Harding to the editor in which Harding addressed several questions directly to Bishop Spalding. He wanted to know, for example, why Spalding had promulgated a pastoral letter on the eve of a national election in which he stated that a great injustice was done to Catholics in compelling them to help support the public schools while their conscience obliged them to maintain their own schools. The *Journal* a week later contained Spalding's reply in which he made it clear that the pastoral letter in question was not his but rather the joint letter of the bishops of the ecclesiastical Province of Chicago. As for Harding's question concerning the prelates' complaints about having to pay taxes to support two school systems, the bishop said:

They hold that freedom of education is involved in freedom of worship and they are opposed to the Edwards Law simply because it is an infringement on their constitutional rights as American citizens. It is unjust to affirm, as you affirm, that Catholics in Wisconsin and in Illinois have made an onslaught on the common schools. No fair-minded and well-informed man will say they have done anything of the kind.[75]

The Bishop's strong attachment to the Germans

and their language prompted him as well to a defense of their loyalty which had been impugned by the Peoria *Journal*. The attempt to cast suspicion on the Germans, whether they be Catholics or Protestants, was described as "an unjust and wanton proceeding," since as a class they were industrious, loyal, and law-abiding citizens, friends of "political and religious freedom," and what Spalding called "the foremost advocates and defenders of a national social liberty. . . ." And in a final fling at the *Journal,* Spalding denied their assertion that Martin Luther was the father of the common school. He stated that Luther had made it clear that he stood for Christian schools, and Spalding contended that schools that excluded religion would have been "an abomination in his eyes." Thus American Lutherans who insisted on their right to parochial schools were only being faithful to Luther's spirit and teaching.

The Catholics had not, indeed, been alone in their opposition to the Edwards Law, since the Lutherans and other Protestant groups had likewise realized its implications for their religious interests. The result was that by the time the political campaign got under way in the fall of 1892 — a campaign in which the Edwards Law figured as a prime issue — the various religious bodies were quite thoroughly aroused. In the November elections the Democrats won a resounding victory in Illinois where they carried not only the governorship with the German-born John P. Altgeld, but also captured both houses of the legislature as well as Illinois' congressional delegation. Early in the new year the new governor and legislature were installed in Springfield and shortly thereafter action was taken to repeal the Edwards Law. In its place a bill was passed in February, 1893, which retained the provision for compulsory education for children between seven and fourteen years of age for at least sixteen weeks a year, but the new law specified that this obligation would be met in "some public or private day school,"[76] language to which no reasonable person could take exception. And with this victory for the private school interests the controversy that had stirred up so much excitement and ill will in Illinois came to an end.

The second controversy over the schools during these same years in which Bishop Spalding figured was not so speedily and decisively snuffed out. One reason was that from the outset it assumed national proportions and included grave disputes among the Catholics themselves as well as attacks on them from without. The situation in brief was this. For some time in a number of American communities Catholic parochial schools had been rented to the local public school boards for a nominal sum such as one dollar a year and had thus become part of the public school system, with teachers' salaries and maintenance of the buildings met from general taxes and with religion taught outside the regular school hours. Poughkeepsie, New York, and Savannah, Georgia, for example, were two places where arrangements of this kind had worked for some years to the general satisfaction of the parties concerned.

In July, 1889, the delegates at the National Education Association's annual meeting, held that year in Nashville, heard a paper written by Cardinal Gibbons as well as a speech by Bishop Keane, Rector of the Catholic University of America. Both men were at pains to explain in a calm and friendly manner the reason for Catholic parochial schools; but their remarks were quickly countered by voices unfriendly to separate religious schools and in the end little would seem to have been gained by the effort. When, therefore, the N.E.A. invited Archbishop Ireland to address their convention the following year in his see city, he determined on a novel approach to enlist the support of this largest and most powerful of all American educational groups for a compromise arrangement between the two school systems along the lines of the so-called Poughkeepsie Plan. His principal intent was to bring the parochial schools closer to the public school system so as to remove all possible basis for regarding the former in any other light than as part of the national educational picture. And he was equally anxious to find relief through this medium for the heavy burden of double support which the Catholic people had to bear for both systems of schools.

Noted for his flamboyant language on occasion,

in this instance the rhetorical flourishes of the Arch-bishop of St. Paul in praise of the public schools, and his brave attempt to have the parochial schools become part of the public educational system, set off a furious quarrel. Violent dissent arose among many of his own coreligionists on the score that his proposals would undermine the parochial schools, just as there was immediate opposition from certain non-Catholic quarters where it was claimed that he was trying to take over the public schools by the back door. Ireland thus found himself beset by both conservative Catholics, to whom he had already given offense by his criticism of the use of foreign languages for teaching in the Catholic schools, and by the A.P.A. and others who were prepared to believe the worst of any Catholic bishop in what-ever relationship he might try to establish with the public schools.[77]

For some years the names of John Lancaster Spalding and John Ireland had been closely linked in a number of important Catholic undertakings such as the colonization association and the university. It was natural, therefore, to expect that they might be united on a subject like the schools in which both took a vital interest. Such, however, was not the case, for there was a wide difference in their views, to say nothing of their methods and approach to the problem. The point can be illus-trated, perhaps by a speech that Spalding gave less than six months after Ireland's address before the

63

N.E.A., when the Bishop of Peoria spoke to the Illinois State Teachers Association at Springfield in the closing days of 1890. Much familiar ground was covered in the first part of the talk in his explanation of why Catholics insisted on religion in the schools. Like Ireland the previous summer, Spalding conceded the right of the State to educate, but he did not accompany his remarks with the lavish praise of the public schools employed by his brother bishop. On the contrary, in his customary forthright manner Spalding criticized the public schools for their failure to recognize religion as the most important element in man's life, and in advocating denominational schools wherein religion would receive its due, he said:

> Our school system then does not rest upon a philosophic view of life and education. We have done what it was easiest to do, not what it was best to do, and in this as in other instances, churchmen have been willing to sacrifice the interests of the nation to the whims of a narrow and jealous temper. The denominational system of popular education is the right system. The secular system is a wrong system.[78]

While Spalding emphasized a number of the same points as Ireland, he was much less irenic in his treatment of the public schools. Yet his speech was carried in the *Educational Review,* the official organ of the N.E.A., and escaped almost entirely the outburst of hostility that had greeted Ireland's address of July, 1890.

The difference is to be accounted for in part by

the contrast in temperament of the two prelates. Both were strong-minded men and both were fearless in the face of opposition. But the brusqueness of Ireland's manner often gave the impression that he was charging head-on, with little regard for the feelings of those involved, while Spalding's cooler and more analytic approach — though in no way mitigating the differences that separated him from his opponents — in the end proved less offensive and was free of the air of a reckless personal attack that left a sting behind it. Actually, Spalding felt alienated by Ireland's methods in a controversy of this kind, and, what was more important, he was fundamentally opposed to the kind of plan that the Archbishop of St. Paul had introduced into the parishes at Faribault and Stillwater, Minnesota, where the parochial schools were rented for one dollar a year to the local public school boards and became a part of that system with religion taught after hours.

When, therefore, after months of public debate among American Catholics over the merits and demerits of the so-called Faribault-Stillwater Plan, it won on April 21, 1892, a decision of toleration from the special commission of cardinals appointed by Pope Leo XIII to investigate the case, the Bishop of Peoria was anything but happy. To Spalding the ideal was embodied in the decrees of the Third Plenary Council of Baltimore that had made parochial schools mandatory in every parish where that was at all feasible,[79] and he had little confidence in the proper execution of the obligation of religious instruction of the young in schools that were part of a public system and that permitted religion to be taught only after the regular school day had closed, or before it opened.

Needless to say, Bishop Spalding felt a certain delicacy about publicly opposing the Faribault-Stillwater Plan. Consequently, in an article on the Catholic educational exhibit at the Chicago exposition that came out three months after Rome's decision, he was at pains to make clear that he was dealing with Catholic education in general and in its relation to the exhibit without, as he said, "any thought of recent controversies, or any desire to offer an expression of opinion on recent utterances of the Propaganda on the subject."[80] In the course of his remarks he did not even mention the *tolerari potest* decree, although it would not be difficult to detect a lack of sympathy for Ireland's plan in the following:

> . . . the Church does not and cannot consent to the exclusion of religion from any educational process. . . . If Catholic children have a right to a Catholic education it follows that the duty devolves upon Catholics to provide the means whereby it may be received; and the Catholics of the United States have accepted the task thus imposed with a spirit of self-sacrifice which is above all praise.[81]

Catholics must not, Spalding maintained, recede from their position; in fact, they could not do so in conscience, and it was especially important to adhere to this principle in an age which was described as witnessing a tendency to remove the school from the Church's control and to give it over to the State in a way that would weaken its religious character.[82]

Nor was Bishop Spalding unduly awed by the arrival in the United States in October of that year of a papal ablegate who, it was said, had been sent in part to see that the decree of the Holy See on the schools was respected in this country. If anything, the presence of Francesco Satolli, titular Archbishop of Lepanto, stiffened Spalding's resistance, and three weeks before the annual meeting of the archbishops was to assemble in New York to hear the ablegate's proposals, he told Archbishop Corrigan:

> It is our plain duty to stand by our Catholic schools now with more courage and firmness than ever before. It is to me simply incredible, incomprehensible how prelates of the Church should imagine that they have found a better way to solve our educational problem than that which commended itself to all the Bishops of the country in the Second and Third Plenary Councils, and which received the Pope's approval. I deplore this tendency to try to unsettle things of the most vital importance upon which hitherto we have all agreed and this disturbance is raised just when we were building more schools than ever before, and making more earnest and successful efforts to improve them.[83]

He was of the opinion that the number of Catholic children allegedly enrolled in non-Catholic schools had been exaggerated, and he saw only one course to pursue, namely, to encourage Catholics to build more schools of their own, and where that was impossible, to insist with both pastors and parents on the urgent need of providing religious instruction for the children in the church and at home.

Meanwhile the four-day meeting of the arch-bishops opened on November 16 at the residence of the Archbishop of New York. More than the usual number of rumors and unverified press stories were circulated about what had gone on in the meeting. But one thing seemed clear, namely, that the fourteen points that the ablegate had submitted to the archbishops on the schools had sustained Ireland's arrangement at Faribault and Stillwater, while at the same time they had tried to safeguard the Baltimore council's legislation. Spalding was deeply disturbed by what he had learned of the New York meeting, and in an interview that appeared in the St. Louis *Chronicle* on December 16 he did not hesitate to speak out with a candor that was characteristic of him. He felt that almost all the bishops were opposed to the plan of the Arch-bishop of St. Paul, that the latter had conceded too much to the State in removing the religious emblems from the parochial classrooms, and that Rome's approval for the schools at Faribault and Stillwater had in no way meant a recommendation of the plan to the rest of the hierarchy. "Archbishop Ireland

and myself are very friendly," he was quoted as saying, "and I do not want to be placed in the position of a critic only so far as my own diocese is concerned when I say I would not permit it." Asked about the high feeling then current in Wisconsin between the German Catholics and their coreligionists of other national backgrounds, Spalding did not pretend to know exactly what the cause was. He alluded to the rift between the ecclesiastical Province of Milwaukee and that of St. Paul that had been separated from it in 1888, remarking that the old fight had not been allowed to die; on the contrary, the two metropolitan sees continued to be centers of quarreling Catholic groups which had caused scandal and it should be made to cease. "I think Archbishop Ireland's desire," he said, "was to force his plan, whatever it is, upon the rest of the country, and that was a mistake on his part. That may be the cause of the continued strife. It would have been better," Spalding concluded, "if the New York Conference had never been held. It only created mischief."

If these words were thought to be very plain speaking, there was more to come before this controversy had run its course. The Bishop of Peoria was genuinely annoyed over Satolli's school propositions, and a lengthy editorial in the *New World* at the end of that year so well expressed his annoyance — if, indeed, it was not his own composition — that he was at pains to send a copy to Archbishop

Corrigan with the remark, "If you think well of it, it might be well to have it reprinted in some of the New York newspapers."[84] The editorial stated that Satolli's proposals were either not practical, or in so far as they were, they had already been adopted in the United States. The Faribault-Stillwater arrangement was declared to be incompatible with the principles of religious education since, according to the writer, it was easy to talk about teaching catechism outside school hours, but it was another thing to put it into practice. As for exhorting Catholic parents to a sense of their duty in this regard, as Archbishop Satolli had urged, that had been done from the beginning in this country. Given this frame of mind, it was to be expected that Spalding would oppose the establishment of the Apostolic Delegation which occurred on January 21, 1893, just three weeks after the appearance of the *New World* editorial. In fact, nearly two years later the bishop was still an outspoken critic of that action, maintaining, in an article written to refute the false charges of the A.P.A., that the hierarchy had not wanted a delegate, and adding that "those whose knowledge of the country was most accurate and intimate believed that the establishment of a papal delegation here would be bad policy."[85]

John Lancaster Spalding's early reputation for courage in stating his convictions remained a distinguishing quality of the man to the end of his life. For example, on the occasion of the dedication on October 13, 1899, of Holy Cross College, the major seminary of the Congregation of Holy Cross adjacent to the Catholic University of America, Spalding was the principal speaker before a large clerical gathering that numbered Cardinal Gibbons, Sebastiano Martinelli, O.S.A., Apostolic Delegate to the United States, and eight other archbishops who were in Washington at the time for the annual meeting of the metropolitans. To those who were accustomed to Spalding's ideas and to the candor with which he expressed them, his pointed remarks about Catholics' failure to be more active in the things of the mind came as no surprise. Nor would anyone have seriously questioned his statement that those who understood the true character of modern thought could not help but realize that Catholicism must "more and more cease to be a power in the world" unless Catholics bestirred themselves and became more intellectually alive.[86]

As was often the case with Spalding, he had generous words on this occasion for his native country and its free institutions, including the separation of Church and State. True, the Church in the United States had no privileges from the State, and if it were to have such, in Spalding's opinion they would harm, not help the Faith. "It is enough," he said, "that we have the rights which in a free country belong to all alike — freedom to teach, to publish, to organize, to worship." Here the Church had an unprecedented opportunity for development, and it was the obligation of American Catholics to make the most of it. And among these advantages the bishop counted the chance to advance the education of women. He alluded to Trinity College, then under construction a few blocks away, as "a monumental witness to our faith" in woman's right to rise to her full stature, to learn whatever was available to be known, and to do whatever she might legitimately find herself able to do.

The speaker then came to a subject that must have been a bit startling to some who were present when he said:

> Those who stand with averted faces looking ever back-ward to Europe do not impress us. What sacredness is there in Europe more than in America? Is not the his-tory of Europe largely a history of wars, tyrannies, oppressions, massacres, and persecutions? . . . Why should Europe be an object of admiration for Catholics? Half its population has revolted from the Church, and in the so-called Catholic nations which are largely gov-erned by atheists, what vital manifestation of religious life and power can we behold?

Regardless of how American Catholics might view Europe, however, their destiny was cast here, and for them to stand in the midst of the advancing modern world with eyes cast backward was to forfeit all chance of influencing the age and of be-ing, as he phrased it, "forever lost as a living force." Emphasizing through a series of questions the unique advantages offered to one who lived in the United States, he made it plain what he thought

72

were the special obligations of Catholics in this free society. "If we fail," said Spalding, "the fault is in ourselves, in our timidity, in our indolence, in our lack of faith. What is there to make us afraid or despondent?"

It was a stirring oration, surely, and it took on special significance when one recalled that this ringing affirmation of belief in and affection for the American way of life came less than a year after Pope Leo XIII's letter *Testem benevolentiae* (January 22, 1899) which was addressed to the hierarchy of this country on the errors grouped under the general heading of 'Americanism.' Spalding's was the kind of talk that was calculated to reassure any American Catholic who might still entertain doubts about the reconcilability of his religious faith and the love he felt for his country and its institutions. In this way he contributed his share in helping to lay the ghost of what was called by some the 'phantom heresy,' even if in doing so he went to extremes at certain moments in his repudiation of Europe, the source from which many of the finest features of American civilization had taken their rise.

Less than six months later the Bishop of Peoria returned to the same theme under still more striking circumstances. Interested as he always was in any cause that would advance the education of the people, while on a visit to Rome he readily responded to an invitation to preach in the Church of the Gesù

73

on March 21, 1900, for the benefit of a free night school which it was proposed to establish in the Eternal City. At the outset of his remarks he declared that the law of man's life was growth; therefore, not only must man himself grow, but so must there be change in the institutions by which his life was sustained and fostered. And this included women as well as men, for the education of women was all important, and if Catholics had failed to win the hearts of all men, it was due, said Spalding, "in no slight degree to our indifference to the education of women."[87] Moreover, in a spirit that was really catholic nothing that was of service to man should be overlooked in the educational process. The bishop made clear his adherence to the principle of authority, but at the same time he believed that man's mind was free and that he had a right to investigate the unknown. If, then, the Catholic Church was to prosper in the contemporary world, said Spalding, "Catholics must have not only freedom to learn, but also freedom to teach."[88]

And in the Church's world of learning men of talent, whether priests or laymen, must be given encouragement to put their intellectual gifts to the highest use, and one way of doing this was to provide for them the best possible schools. For if Catholics isolated themselves and withdrew from the circles where the thought of the modern world was being shaped, in Spalding's judgment, they

74

would drift into a position of inferiority and lose whatever chance they might have to make themselves heard and understood. For example, in the field of historical research there should be no dread of what would be unearthed about the defects of the Church's members, for the cockle often grows with the wheat and, as the bishop put it, "what God has permitted to happen, man may be permitted to know. . . ."[89] In fact, if one had the wisdom to perceive it, lessons of lasting value could be gleaned from this sort of knowledge.

At this point Spalding entered upon a spirited defense of those who by virtue of the originality of their thought or the fruits of their research broke new ground and advanced the frontiers of knowledge in their respective fields. Theirs was the kind of life, he maintained, that required a discipline, courage, and self-denial that were given only to the few. When, therefore, men of this caliber devoted their lives to the elucidation of the doctrines of religion, "we must honor and trust them," he said, "or they will lose heart or turn to studies in which their labors will be appreciated." In a further elaboration of the point he continued:

> If mistrust of our ablest minds be permitted to exist, the inevitable result will be a lowering of the whole intellectual life of Catholics, and as a consequence a lowering of their moral and religious life. If we have no great masters, how shall we hope to have eager and loving disciples? If we have no men who write vital books — books of power, books which are literature

75

and endure — how shall we expect to enter along an inner line into the higher life of the age, to quicken, purify, and exalt the hopes and thoughts of men?[90]

He then gave the Bible as an illustration of a work that was often the basis of serious misunderstandings by theologians themselves; and since the inspired writers of Scripture had thus been easily misunderstood, was it not a duty, Spalding asked, "to treat with good will and loving kindness authors who, not being supernaturally assisted," employed their God-given talents through tireless industry to illumine old truths with the light of new knowledge such as the modern mind possesses?

Bishop Spalding would thus give the greatest possible liberty to the Church's scholars, for only when they were unhampered in their quest for the widest and deepest knowledge could they fulfill the role which was expected of them. In this Spalding saw, as few churchmen of his generation, the necessity for the broadest intellectual freedom, and for that reason the tendency that he encountered among certain ecclesiastics made him apprehensive of the future of Catholicism lest the ultraconservative views of these men acquire a preponderant influence in the Church. He knew, too, as few of his kind in that opening year of the new century, the main lines of development in secular circles, and for that reason he was extremely anxious to bring Catholic thinking abreast of modern thought in order that it might exert an influence on the men of his own generation. One almost senses an uneasiness in the bishop's mind, for example, in a passage such as the following:

> To forbid men to think along whatever line, is to place oneself in opposition to the deepest and most invincible tendency of the civilized world. Were it possible to compel obedience from Catholics in matters of this kind, the result would be a hardening and sinking of our whole religious life. We should more and more drift away from the vital movements of the age, and find ourselves at last immured in a spiritual ghetto, where no man can breathe pure air, or be joyful or strong or free.[91]

In his attempt to win a hearing for the best educational training for the Catholic clergy, Spalding invoked certain names that would be familiar to his Roman audience. He quoted Rosmini, for example, as saying that one of the five wounds from which the Church suffered was the inferior professors to whom were entrusted the training of future priests, those who were to be the guides and models of the multitude. Likewise the learned Josef Cardinal Hergenröther, who had died ten years before, was cited to the effect that no greater pleasure could be given the deadliest enemies of the Church, "than by destroying the theological faculty of any university, or by calling away from it its ecclesiastical students."[92] But intellectual advancement among the clergy needed more than universities; it also called for constant self-criticism and re-evaluation of one's educational efforts,

77

Ceaseless vigilance was not the price of liberty alone, said Spalding; it was the price one had to pay for all spiritual good. How, then, he asked, can men be ever vigilant, "if we are forbidden to criticize ourselves and the environment by which our life is nourished and protected"?[93]

In conclusion the Bishop of Peoria stated that he had spoken as an American Catholic, a viewpoint which, he thought, was that of most of the English-speaking world with its similarity of political and social institutions. And in this world where the English language prevailed everywhere there was freedom to write, to publish, and to discuss, nor was it possible "to fence about and shut in from the all-searching breath of liberty" any subject or interest. This was the existing condition of things, and there was every indication that it would continue:

> It is a state of things English-speaking Catholics accept without mental reservations, without misgivings, without regrets, which are always idle; and the common rights which are ours in the midst of a general freedom, have stirred in us an energy of thought and action, which have led to triumphs and conquests that have not been achieved by Catholics elsewhere in the wonderful century that is now closing.[94]

In many ways "Education and the Future of Religion," as Spalding entitled his Roman sermon of March, 1900, was his most notable pulpit performance. Delivered at a time when the memory of all informed men was still alive with the subject of Americanism, it constituted a bold challenge to those who seemed determined to find doctrinal errancy among the American Catholics. In no way did the preacher run counter to the warnings and cautions sounded by Leo XIII's *Testem benevolentiae* of a year and two months before. Yet Spalding succeeded in reaffirming his own personal faith in the favored position of the Church of the United States and other English-speaking countries, as well as making about as emphatic a plea for intellectual freedom as one will find in the literature of the American Church. The sermon drew considerable attention when it was first published in brochure form by the Ave Maria Press and later reprinted in one of the bishop's books. The leading Protestant weekly of the United States made it the subject of an enthusiastic editorial in which it was said, "For the intelligence, courage and sound Americanism of this admirable sermon Catholics and Protestants may equally be grateful. Such a leader, who is scholar, theologian and poet, is an honor to his Church."[95]

We have several times mentioned Spalding's promotion of education for women. He spoke of it frequently, and that at a time when it was still regarded as a rather advanced idea in the sense that there were relatively few enthusiasts for the cause among his coreligionists, while Americans in general were far from converted to the notion that women should have equal advantages for higher education with men. But as in other matters, once Spalding became convinced of the validity of an idea he had no hesitation in expounding it even if it brought little response. The address at the dedication of the Holy Cross Fathers' major seminary was not the first time that he had upheld the hands of Sister Euphrasia Taylor and her companion Sisters of Notre Dame de Namur who were struggling against considerable odds to establish Trinity College for girls in Washington. Almost a year before he had given a lecture in the national capital with a view to gaining public support for the college. Talented women, he stated on that occasion, should be given an opportunity for advanced training the same as men. In any category of humanity, said Spalding, the really superior minds were only a small minority, but the contribution that they made to society far outweighed in value their meager numbers. "For it is they," the bishop remarked, "who uplift the ideals in whose light the multitude walk — it is they who open ways to undiscovered worlds — it is they who show to the crowd what right hoping and right doing of human souls may achieve."[96]

Language of this kind sounds somewhat banal today when applied to higher education for women. But it was anything but an accepted fact in Catholic circles in the 1890's when, for example, the mere rumor of a college for girls near the Catholic University of America was sufficient to bring an anxious inquiry to the Archbishop of Baltimore from Cardinal Satolli, Prefect of the Congregation of Studies, who stated that the newspaper accounts of the project had made a "disagreeable impression" in Rome, where it had been described as "a dangerous addition and amalgamation of Institutions, for the teaching of students of both sexes."[97] Fortunately, like Spalding, Cardinal Gibbons believed that such an institution was highly desirable, and he made that fact known in his reply to Satolli, as well as to the latter's successor as Apostolic Delegate to the United States when Archbishop Martinelli wrote in the same fretful vein.[98] The plans continued to move forward, therefore, and no Catholic churchman was happier than Spalding when the difficulties had all been overcome and Trinity College was formally opened on November 7, 1900, for the nineteen young ladies who constituted its pioneer student body.

In line with Bishop Spalding's support of Trinity College was his early advocacy of an institution in the neighborhood of the Catholic University of America where the members of the religious congregations of women whose principal work was teaching might receive proper training for their work. Here again the idea was far from a popular one when first made known, and time was needed for it to take hold in the minds of the responsible parties. Happily, a special advocate was at hand soon after the turn of the century in Father Thomas

E. Shields, a priest of the Archdiocese of St. Paul, who had come to the university in 1902 to teach psychology. Shields became a highly articulate promoter of a training school for the sisters, and he found his problem "partially solved," as it was said, by an outline that Spalding had worked out for such an institution some years before. The prestige of the Bishop of Peoria in the end proved a powerful help to Shields who, as his biographer remarked, "could have found no better backing for his plan. . . ."[99] It was Spalding's original outline, then, with some modifications, that formed the basis of the proposals presented to Pope Pius X who gave the project his blessing. In the sequel the university trustees were finally brought around, financial backing was assured, and in October, 1911, the Sisters College of the Catholic University of America opened its doors.

Still another educational undertaking of national scope in which much was owed to Spalding was the Catholic Educational Exhibit at the World's Columbian Exposition of 1893. At the request of the archbishops he agreed to act as president of the hierarchy's committee, an assignment that involved the supervision of arrangements for the numerous exhibits sent in by dioceses, religious orders, and individual institutions, and which were assembled under the immediate direction of Brother Maurelian Schell, F.S.C. When the metropolitans held their annual meeting in Chicago in September, 1893, they were obviously pleased with the result, and as a token of their appreciation a resolution was passed which stated that they wished to recognize the services rendered to the American Church by Spalding in having consented to assume the responsibility for the work and, they added, "in having guided this undertaking to a successful issue by his wisdom, prudence and skill."[100]

In addition to these various educational enterprises the Bishop of Peoria had meanwhile continued since 1884 to serve as one of the most informed and helpful members of the Board of Trustees of the national university. A stroke of paralysis in 1905, however, greatly impaired his movements, and after he realized that he would no longer be able to play an active role, he asked in the spring of 1907 that his resignation be accepted. Cardinal Gibbons informed the bishop of the reluctance with which the trustees had assented to his request, assured him of their gratitude for all that he had done for the university from the beginning, and stated that the trustees recognized that in a sense, as he put it, "you could be considered its founder and its ever-constant protector."[101] Thus Spalding was not solely the educational theorist, as was evidenced by his work for the Catholic University of America, his practical assistance to a number of women's institutions, and to the exhibit at the Chicago world's fair, to say nothing of the way in which he built up the educational system of his own diocese.

Of the norms by which posterity seeks to evaluate a man's contribution to any cause, the judgment of his contemporaries and the opinion of professionals and specialists of a later day are, perhaps, the most generally accepted. In the context of the history of American education John Lancaster Spalding has fared well at the hands of both groups. Enough has been said about the esteem he enjoyed among his contemporaries, for by 1880 he was on the way to establishing himself as the most authoritative voice on educational matters among American Catholics, and most of his coreligionists, including many of his fellow bishops, turned to him for leadership and guidance. Few men of the period would seriously gainsay, therefore, a writer in the *Independent* who in 1893 spoke of Spalding as "by far the most scholarly and cultured man in the hierarchy," even if some might have reservations about his "cold intellectuality" being unrelieved by the energy and enthusiasm of men like Ireland and Keane.[102]

Moreover, esteem for Spalding's educational achievements was not confined to Catholic circles. For example, both Western Reserve University and Columbia University chose the Bishop of Peoria as the recipient of an honorary degree. And when Nicholas Murray Butler, the President of Columbia, announced to the bishop the action of the university trustees, his statement of what they had in mind in unanimously voting him the degree summarized in a few words what Spalding had come to stand for in the minds of many Americans, namely, "eminence and service as a Christian priest and Bishop, as scholar, and man of letters, as educator and citizen."[103]

Several decades after his death the critical judgment of professional educators on Spalding's work began to appear in a considerable number of studies wherein the general appreciation expressed was uniformly high. Two of these studies will illustrate what is meant. One was a volume by a Belgian priest educator, Franz de Hovre, that came out in 1930. It consisted of a series of essays on outstanding Catholic figures in the world of education such as Cardinal Newman for England, Félix Dupanloup, Bishop of Orleans, for France, and Spalding, who was de Hovre's choice to represent the United States. The author confessed that he could find no systematic philosophy of education in Spalding's works except, of course, the strong emphasis on Christian moral values. But he saw in the bishop's aim of bridging the gap that separated "American ways of thinking from Catholic ideals,"[104] a highly commendable idea. To de Hovre one of the chief merits of Spalding as an educator lay in his insistence on the social aspects of education, that is, as to its origins, content, organization, and external forms, while the personal was served through its ideals, spirit, and inspiration.[105] Spalding's frequent mention of the importance of character formation in the educative process was noted as well as his advancement of higher education for women, and in conclusion de Hovre described him as "an apostle of encouragement to those engaged in the work of teaching," and declared that in this sense the Bishop of Peoria deserved to rank with "the great masters in the field of Catholic Education."[106]

The second symposium on outstanding educators in which Spalding figured as the representative of the American Catholics was published several years after de Hovre's book and was written by a non-Catholic professor of American social history. Merle Curti rightly sensed the value for estimating Spalding's place in the educational picture of his own generation that attached to the judgment of William T. Harris, who from 1889 to 1906 occupied the office of United States Commissioner of Education, one who, as it has recently been said, was the man who "ultimately rationalized the institution of the public school."[107] Harris' admiration for Spalding was manifest in his introduction of him to a Washington audience in 1899 as "the most beloved of American educational leaders." And it was the bishop's insistence on the fact that man had been made to the image and likeness of God and possessed an immortal soul, that Harris found especially worthy of commendation.[108]

In his own analysis of Spalding's educational endeavors, Professor Curti saw him as a pioneer in the promoting of teacher training, as a stalwart advocate of Americanization for his foreign-born coreligionists — although here he stood for a more gradual process than Archbishop Ireland — and as one who did much to bring the Catholic community in this country abreast of modern trends and ideas. "Bishop Spalding, in short," he said, "brought Catholic education from the narrow confines of race and language to the broad platform of Christian teaching."[109] The bishop's constant emphasis on religious values and moral character was noted, but, said Curti, it was an emphasis that in no way did violence to the cultivation of the intellectual virtues. Spalding's comments on American society, and his frequently acute observations about certain of its weaknesses, were seen as a constructive force since the bishop's fundamental love for his country was beyond question. And the fact that he did not permit his deep abhorrence of socialism to blind him to the abuses of the capitalist system or to labor's claims for justice, was to Curti a very attractive feature of Spalding's contribution to social betterment. President Theodore Roosevelt's choice of the Bishop of Peoria in 1902 as a member of the anthracite coal commission for adjudicating the strike of the miners was adduced as testimony of the regard in which he was held, and by his general defense of the rights of labor he won, in the judgment of Curti, not only a lasting place in the memory of the workingman but a place among the "small and exceptional group of educators which includes Margaret Haley and John Dewey."[110] But what would have pleased Spalding, I believe, more than anything else in the Curti essay was the judgment that during this period no one had contributed more "to convince Catholics, and even Protestants, that the parochial school could provide a secular education equal to that which prevailed in the best public institutions."[111]

Others besides Professor Curti were attracted by Spalding's efforts to enlighten public opinion concerning the plight of the American workingman. At a time when the bishop was at the height of his prestige he caught the attention of a young Minnesota-born priest who began to read him and to follow his activities. That priest was the future Monsignor John A. Ryan, professor of moral theology in the Catholic University of America, whose later fame was as widespread as Spalding's own. In his memoirs Ryan spoke of five or six men who had helped to shape his thinking as a young man, and among these was Spalding, whom he described as "undoubtedly the greatest literary artist in the entire history of the American hierarchy."[112] He stated that for many years Spalding exercised what he called "a greater influence upon my general philosophy of life, my ideals, my sense of comparative values than any other contemporary writer."[113] Coming from a man of Ryan's stature, this was high praise, indeed. One of the things that made an especially deep impression on him was Spalding's eloquent panegyric at a memorial meeting in April, 1902, for John P. Altgeld, former Governor of Illinois, who had died a month before. Two years later, said Ryan, the Bishop of Peoria was a guest of Archbishop Ireland of St. Paul who accompanied him to a reception in his honor at St. Paul Seminary. Ryan was seated only a few feet away from the two prelates, and he stated that when one of the speakers on the program announced that his contribution would be a reading of the Illinois bishop's panegyric of Altgeld, Ireland, who had not fancied the late governor, "made an exclamation of surprise and dissent." Thereupon Spalding was said to have promptly and vigorously retorted, "The best thing I ever wrote!"[114] The exchange was an interesting reflection of the views of the two principals, as it was characteristic of the many differences that obtained between them during their nearly forty years of close association.

The notable service rendered by the Bishop of Peoria to the educational progress of both his Church and his country was in good measure terminated in 1905 when, as has been mentioned, he suffered the first of a series of strokes. But he had already achieved a remarkable record, one such as few American churchmen of any religious faith have ever known. For eleven years he lived on in the city that he had come to love, comforted by the

kindly attention of members of his family and con-
soled by the intellectual delights that he had cultivated through a lifetime, and about which many
years before he had said:

> Time only increases their charm, and in the winter of
> age, when the body is but the agent of pain, contempla-
> tion still remains like the light of a higher world, to
> tinge with beauty the clouds that gather around life's
> setting.[115]

No member of the American Catholic community, clerical or lay, had ever given a more complete and consistent fulfillment to the mandate of
Christ that one should let his light shine before the
men of his generation[116] than the first Bishop of
Peoria. And by reason of that fact Americans of
his and later generations have been the more en-
riched by his sharing the superior gifts of his mind
and heart. If one were seeking for a fitting summa-
tion of the career of John Lancaster Spalding as an
educator, he could hardly improve upon the words
addressed to him in 1913 by John J. Glennon,
Archbishop of St. Louis, on the occasion of his
golden jubilee as a priest. Glennon struck an altogether happy note in describing Spalding as "the
one Catholic who has best understood the American mind," and in endeavoring to explain how
that central fact had colored much of what the aged
prelate had accomplished for both Church and
State, he said:

> He has understood it because in all wherein it was best,

it was his own. He has understood it, because he has approached the study in a broad, generous and Catholic way. And knowing it, he did not fear it; and because of the love of it, and because it was his duty he would instruct and elevate it, he would Catholicize it. And so in season and out of season, with voice and pen, he struggled to edify, enlighten and conquer for Christ the hearts and minds of his fellow countrymen. At length his strength gave way; his hand would hold the pen no longer; and he, the athlete of Christ, was compelled to rest. But, the impress he made and the good he has accomplished (again unequaled in the annals of our American Church), remains in all its unfading richness at once his consolation and his crown.[117]

NOTES

* On October 25, 1960, the writer spoke on the educational contributions of Bishop Spalding at a solemn pontifical Mass in St. Mary's Cathedral, Peoria, Illinois. The Mass was a feature of the annual meeting of the School Superintendents' Department of the National Catholic Educational Association. At the suggestion of the Right Reverend Frederick G. Hochwalt, Executive Secretary of the Association, the sermon on that occasion was expanded and adapted to meet the requirements of the Gabriel Richard Lecture for 1961. The writer wishes to express his sincere thanks to his student and friend, the Reverend David F. Sweeney, O.F.M., of St. Francis College, Rye Beach, New Hampshire, for his generosity and kindness in putting at his disposal a number of references from his doctoral dissertation, "The Life of John Lancaster Spalding, First Bishop of Peoria, 1840–1916," which is nearing completion, and, too, for his critical reading of the manuscript of this present work. He is likewise grateful to his friend, the Very Reverend Louis A. Arand, S.S., associate professor of dogmatic theology in The Catholic University of America, who has once again done him the favor of giving the typescript of this work a close and critical reading.

1. *Ceremonies of the Golden Sacerdotal Jubilee of His Grace John Lancaster Spalding, Titular Archbishop of Sciotopolis* (Chicago, 1913), p. 31.

2. *Souvenir of the Episcopal Silver Jubilee of the Rt. Rev. J. L. Spalding, D.D., Bishop of Peoria* (Chicago, 1903), p. 25.

3. A striking example of eagerness for learning on the part of an American youth in a frontier environment similar to that of Lebanon is found in the recent work of Paul Horgan, *Citizen of New Salem* (New York, 1961), which recounts with great charm Abraham Lincoln's six years in New Salem, the Illinois village that he left for Springfield in 1837, three years before Spalding was born.

4. Peter Verhaegen, S.J., to Benedict Spalding, December 5, 1849, quoting Martin J. Spalding, Coadjutor Bishop of Louisville, on St. Mary's, in Gilbert J. Garraghan, S.J., *The Jesuits of the Middle United States* (New York, 1938), III, 305.

5. *Alumni News* [St. Mary's College] (Spring, 1958), 5.

6. A number of Spalding's letters from his student days

are preserved among the manuscript collections at the University of Notre Dame. In 1943 the writer secured photostat copies of the originals and edited them — along with Spalding letters from other collections — under the title "Some Student Letters of John Lancaster Spalding," *Catholic Historical Review*, XXIX (January, 1944), 510–539. Hereafter reference will be made to the originals at Notre Dame by use of the symbol UND followed by the customary details of names and dates with the page on which they can be found in the printed copy. Thus for the letter to Mrs. Spalding referred to above: UND, Spalding to his mother, Emmitsburg, November 11, 1857 (p. 511).

7. UND, same to same, Emmitsburg, December 2, 1857 (p. 512).

8. Mary M. Meline and Edward F. X. McSweeney, *The Story of the Mountain* (Emmitsburg, 1911), I, 528. Actually, the search of the boys' boxes was prompted by the discovery of what was called "an obscene book," and it was the protest of the students against having their boxes searched by the prefects without first asking for their keys like "gentlemen," that set off the "rebellion" when Dr. McCaffrey, the president of the college, refused to accede to the students' demands.

9. *Ibid.*, I, 529.

10. Michael J. Kelly and James M. Kirwin, *History of Mt. St. Mary's Seminary of the West, Cincinnati, Ohio* (Cincinnati, 1894), p. 90. Probably the most memorable event of Spalding's year in Cincinnati was the celebration in October, 1858, of Purcell's silver jubilee as a bishop at which the students assisted.

11. M. J. Spalding to Kenrick, Florence, March 6, 1853, in John D. Sauter, *The American College of Louvain (1857–1898)* (Louvain, 1959), p. 19.

12. Archives of the Archdiocese of Baltimore, 37-E-13, Martin Spalding to his brother Richard, Louisville, Christmas Eve, 1859. Hereafter these archives will be referred to as AAB.

13. David Russell (1830–1900) was in 1858 the first native American student to enter the American College at Louvain. He was ordained there on December 22, 1860, and after several years of parish work in the Diocese of Louisville he returned to the college where he was vice-rector and professor of English during the academic year 1865–1866.

14. AAB, 37-E-14, Martin Spalding to his brother Richard, Louisville, December 30, 1859.

15. *Annuaire de l'Université catholique de Louvain, 1865* (Louvain, 1865), p. 192. On the same day the Belgian-born Henry Gabriels, a future Bishop of Ogdensburg, New York, received the S.T.L. degree, and Patrick W. Riordan of Chicago, destined to be Archbishop of San Francisco, received his S.T.B. Both this issue of the *Annuaire* and that of 1863 mention Spalding as being from the Diocese of St. Louis.

16. UND, Spalding to his parents, Louvain, August 12, 1862 (p. 515).

17. J. Van der Heyden, *The Louvain American College* (Louvain, 1909), p. 86.

18. An excellent brief survey of Belgian religious affairs at this time may be found in Roger Aubert, *Le pontificat de Pie IX, 1846–1878* (Paris, 1952), pp. 163–171.

19. AAB, 37-A-1, Spalding to Martin Spalding, Louvain, April 2, 1861 (p. 518).

20. AAB, 37-A-2, Spalding to David Russell, Louvain, December 6, 1862 (p. 519). As Spalding taught English, so another student who was to be an American bishop, Charles J. Seghers [Archbishop of Oregon City] was then teaching music.

21. UND, Spalding to his parents, Louvain, May 3, 1864 (p. 524).

22. UND, same to same, Freiburg, July 24, 1864 (p. 526).

23. AAB, 37-A-5, Spalding to Archbishop Spalding, Venice, September 19, 1864 (p. 527).

24. *Ibid.*

25. AAB, 37-A-6, same to same, Rome, November 15, 1864.

26. AAB, 37-A-7, same to same, Rome, January 5, 1865.

27. AAB, Letterbook of Archbishop Spalding, p. 506, Martin Spalding to Spalding, Baltimore, February 16, 1865 (p. 535).

28. AAB, 37-A-8, Spalding to Martin Spalding, Rome, March 13, 1865 (p. 538).

29. AAB, 37-E-40, Martin Spalding to Spalding, Baltimore, July 26, 1865 (p. 539).

30. UND, Purcell Papers, McCloskey to Purcell, Louisville, January 23, 1869. The writer owes this reference as well as those in Notes 74, 75, 83, 84, and 103 to the Sweeney manuscript mentioned in the introductory note.

31. AAB, Letterbook of Archbishop Spalding, p. 150. Martin Spalding to John Timon, Baltimore, August 23, 1865. The substance of this and other letters on the university question can be found in the writer's volume, *The Formative Years of the Catholic University of America* (Washington, 1946), p. 45 ff.

32. Spalding, *The Life of the Most Rev. M. J. Spalding, Archbishop of Baltimore* (New York, 1873), pp. 313–317.

33. *Ibid.,* p. 304.

34. In 1881 the Diocese of Peoria was enlarged by having added to it from the Archdiocese of Chicago the following counties: Bureau, LaSalle, Henry, Putnam, and Rock Island.

35. *Sadlier's Catholic Directory, Almanac and Ordo . . . 1878* (New York, 1878), pp. 339–341, and the same publication for the following year, p. 345. That the statistics in these volumes are not to be taken as altogether accurate would seem to be obvious from the fact that the estimated 45,000 Catholics of 1878 in the Diocese of Peoria jumped to an estimated 60,000 by 1879. True, Catholic immigration into Illinois in the 1870's was very considerable, but it is doubtful if it was that rapid.

36. *Official Catholic Directory . . . 1908* (New York, 1908), p. 525.

37. On this movement cf. Sister Mary Evangela Henthorne, B.V.M., *The Irish Catholic Colonization Association of the United States* (Champaign, 1932).

38. James P. Shannon, *Catholic Colonization on the Western Frontier* (New Haven, 1957), p. 75.

39. Spalding, *The Religious Mission of the Irish People and Catholic Colonization* (New York, 1880), p. 13.

40. *Ibid.,* p. 122.

41. The devastating effects of the Purcell failure are told in John H. Lamott, *History of the Archdiocese of Cincinnati, 1821–1921* (New York, 1921), pp. 189–207.

42. Archives of the Archdiocese of Cincinnati, Spalding to Elder, Peoria, August 29, 1880, printed in Ellis, *Formative Years,* pp. 68–69.

43. Ellis, *op. cit.,* p. 77.

44. *Ibid.,* p. 78.

45. *Ibid.,* p. 79.

46. *Lectures and Discourses* (New York, 1882). It is entitled here "The Catholic Priesthood," pp. 127–160.

47. AAB, 76-A-8, Spalding to Gibbons, Peoria, July 18, 1882.

48. The principal items in the periodicals and press, as well as in the bishops' letters, are summarized in Ellis, *op., cit.,* pp. 76–86.

49. Archives of the Diocese of Rochester, Hennessy to Mc-Quaid, Jersey City, November 10, 1882.

50. *Ibid.,* McQuaid to Gilmour, Rochester, February 27, 1883, copy.

51. Spalding to De Nève, n.d., n.p., Van der Heyden, *op. cit.,* pp. 173–174.

52. The text of the sermon was published in Spalding's *Means and Ends of Education* (Chicago, 1895) under the title "The Higher Education," pp. 181–232.

53. *Ibid.,* pp. 212–213.

54. *Ibid.,* p. 231.

55. *Address of the Rt. Rev. J. L. Spalding, Bishop of Peoria, delivered at the Laying of the Cornerstone of the Catholic University of America, May 24, 1888* (Peoria, 1888), pp. 6–7.

56. Cf., especially the letters of September 19, 1864, from Venice and January 5, 1865, from Rome [AAB, 37-A-5 and 37-A-7] in the *Catholic Historical Review,* XXIX (January, 1944), 527–529; 532–535.

57. *Address . . . at the Laying of the Cornerstone . . . ,* p. 25.

58. Archives of the Archdiocese of New York, 1–42, Simeoni to Corrigan, Rome, April 8, 1889. Hereafter these archives will be designated as AANY.

59. Martin Grabmann, *Thomas Aquinas. His Personality and Thought.* Translated by Virgil Michel, O.S.B. (New York, 1928), pp. 9–11. St. John Fisher was also an innovator in using his influence to have the statutes of Christ's College, Cambridge, include a study of the poets and orators of antiquity who were then relatively unknown, and insisting that the students of St. John's College which he founded at Cambridge in 1516, should master Greek and Hebrew in order to read the Scriptures in the original languages, an "innovation" which Fisher did not hesitate to undertake personally when nearly fifty years of age. Cf. E. E. Reynolds, *Saint John Fisher* (London, 1955), p. 29 ff.

60. UND, Hudson Papers, Spalding to Daniel Hudson, C.S.C., Peoria, August 26, 1898, photostat. For the case of Keane, cf. Patrick H. Ahern, *The Life of John J. Keane,*

Educator and Archbishop, 1839–1918 (Milwaukee, 1955), p. 120 ff.

61. Ellis, *op. cit.,* pp. 157–158.

62. Archives of The Catholic University of America, "Memorial of John J. Keane," pp. 4–5.

63. Cf., note 47.

64. *Ceremonies of the Golden Sacerdotal Jubilee . . . ,* p. 44.

65. James Cardinal Gibbons, "Silver Jubilee of the Catholic University, April 15, 1915," *A Retrospect of Fifty Years* (Baltimore, 1916), II, 195.

66. *Essays and Reviews* (New York, 1877). Spalding stated in the preface to this volume that its contents had appeared "with one or two exceptions, substantially as they are here published, in the *Catholic World* during the last eighteen months" (p. 5).

67. "The Catholic Church in the United States, 1776–1876," *Catholic World,* XXIII (July, 1876), 452. The same essay was carried in *Essays and Reviews,* pp. 9–49.

68. For a recent discussion of this question, cf. Sister Marie Carolyn Klinkhamer, O.P., "The Blaine Amendment of 1875: Private Motives for Political Action," *Catholic Historical Review,* XLII (April, 1956), 15–49. That Catholics were not free from sectarian and exaggerated reactions to certain phases of the school question may be seen in John Whitney Evans, "Catholics and the Blair Education Bill," *Catholic Historical Review,* XLVI (October, 1960), 273–298.

69. "Normal Schools for Catholics," *Catholic World,* LI (April, 1890), 89. To Spalding virtually all of the nation's problems would yield to the remedies that education had to offer. For example, in response to Leo XIII's encyclical, *Rerum novarum,* of May 15, 1891, he wrote an article in which he scored the brutalization of men by the industrial process, repudiated the theories of Marx and Ricardo as true remedies, and confessed that Catholics had at least this much in common with Socialists that they both deplored the system that landed immigrants on American shores in such a pitiful condition. Here, too, the defects of the capitalist order would be corrected best through education such as the advances of science would bring by way of a greater knowledge of the causes of mankind's distress and thus a remedy through hygiene and sanitation. "We shall make education universal," he said, "but we shall educate

with a view to health of body and soul quite as much, at least, as with a view to sharpen the mental faculties." "Socialism and Labor," *Catholic World,* LIII (September, 1891), 807.

70. For the Edwards Law, cf. Daniel W. Kucera, O.S.B., *Church-State Relationships in Education in Illinois* (Washington, 1955), pp. 111–133.
   On the Bennett Law, cf. Louise Phelps Kellogg, "The Bennett Law in Wisconsin," *Wisconsin Magazine of History,* II (September, 1918), 3–25.

71. An editorial of March 15, 1890.

72. "The Catholic Educational Exhibit in the Columbian Exposition," *Catholic World,* LV (July, 1892), 581.

73. *Ibid.,* p. 584.

74. *New World,* September 10, 1892, photostat. The writer wishes to thank the Reverend Bartholomew F. Fair of St. Charles Borromeo Seminary, Philadelphia, for his kindness in furnishing a photostat of this particular issue of the Chicago Catholic weekly, as well as for his generosity in supplying a microfilm copy of the first two years of the *New World.* Another feature of Illinois Catholicism besides the *New World* that owed its origin to the controversy over the Edwards Law was the amalgamation of a number of German Catholic societies into the Katholischer Vereinsbund von Illinois organized in a meeting at Peoria in 1893, with one of its principal objectives to keep an eye on state legislation and its relation to Catholic interests.

75. Peoria *Journal,* October 20, 1892. The writer wishes to thank his friend, the Reverend John J. Sweeney, Superintendent of Schools of the Diocese of Peoria, for his kindness in checking this reference for him on the microfilm copy in the Peoria Public Library. He is likewise obligated to Miss Elizabeth Hilderbrand, Reference Librarian of the Peoria Public Library, for checking items in the Peoria *Journal.*

76. Kucera, *op. cit.,* p. 126.

77. The most extensive treatment of this episode will be found in Daniel F. Reilly, O.P., *The School Controversy, 1891–1893* (Washington, 1943). For the text of the controversial address cf. Ireland's *The Church and Modern Society* (St. Paul, 1905), I, 215–232.

78. "Religious Instruction in State Schools," *Educational Review,* II (July, 1891), 121. This speech was also pub-

lished in Spalding's *Means and Ends of Education* (Chicago, 1909), pp. 151–180.

79. On the legislation of 1884 on parochial schools cf. Francis P. Cassidy, "Catholic Education in the Third Plenary Council of Baltimore," *Catholic Historical Review,* XXIV (October, 1948), 292–297.

80. "The Catholic Educational Exhibit in the Columbian Exposition," *Catholic World,* LV (July, 1892), 580.

81. *Ibid.,* p. 581.

82. *Ibid.,* p. 584.

83. AANY, C-4, Spalding to Corrigan, Peoria, October 25, 1892.

84. AANY, C-4, Same to same, Peoria, December 30, 1892. The editorial in the *New World* of December 31, 1892, was entitled "Agitating for a Delegate," and was intended to refute a recent editorial in the *Northwestern Chronicle,* Catholic weekly of St. Paul, advocating the establishment of an apostolic delegation.

85. "Catholicism and APAism," *North American Review,* CLIX (September, 1894), 282–293. For a general treatment of the delegation question, cf. John Tracy Ellis, *The Life of James Cardinal Gibbons, Archbishop of Baltimore, 1834–1921* (Milwaukee, 1952), I, 595–652.

86. *Church News* (Washington), October 14, 1899. The text of Spalding's talk was also carried in the *Catholic University Bulletin,* V (October, 1899), 463–486, under the title, "The University: A Nursery of the Higher Life."

87. The text of the Gesù sermon was published by Spalding in *Religion, Agnosticism and Education* (Chicago, 1902), pp. 147–192. The reference to women's education will be found on pages 152–153.

88. *Ibid.,* p. 158.

89. *Ibid.,* p. 160.

90. *Ibid.,* pp. 163–164.

91. *Ibid.,* p. 175.

92. *Ibid.,* pp. 178–179.

93. *Ibid.,* p. 183.

94. *Ibid.,* pp. 188–189.

95. "Bishop Spalding on Americanism," *The Independent,* LII (September 20, 1900), 2287.

96. "Women and the Higher Education," *Mosher's Magazine* (February, 1899), 249–250.

97. Satolli to Gibbons, Rome, August 15, 1897, in Peter E. Hogan, S.S.J., *The Catholic University of America, 1896–1903. The Rectorship of Thomas J. Conaty* (Washington, 1949), p. 97.

98. Martinelli to Gibbons, Atlantic City, August 23, 1897, *ibid.*, p. 97. Gibbons' replies to Satolli and Martinelli are given in Hogan, *op. cit.*, pp. 97–98.

99. Justine Ward, *Thomas Edward Shields, Biologist, Psychologist, Educator* (New York, 1947), pp. 190–191.

100. *Catalogue, Catholic Educational Exhibit. World's Columbian Exposition* (Chicago, 1893), p. 3.

101. AAB, 104-F, Gibbons to Spalding, Baltimore, April 30, 1907, copy.

102. Mervin-Marie Snell, "Pen-Pictures of the American Hierarchy," *The Independent,* XLV (April 27, 1893), 566.

103. Archives of Columbia University, Butler to Spalding, New York, May 6, 1902, copy.

104. Franz de Hovre, *Catholicism in Education.* Translated by Edward B. Jordan (New York, 1934), p. 167. The original edition of this work was entitled *Le Catholicisme. Ses Pédagogues. Sa Pédagogie* (Brussels, 1930).

105. *Ibid.,* p. 183.

106. *Ibid.,* p. 195.

107. Lawrence A. Cremin, *The Transformation of the School. Progressivism in American Education: 1876–1957* (New York, 1961), p. 15.

108. Merle Curti, *The Social Ideas of American Educators* (New York, 1935), p. 348.

109. *Ibid.,* p. 355.

110. *Ibid.,* p. 367.

111. *Ibid.,* p. 356.

112. John A. Ryan, *Social Doctrine in Action. A Personal History* (New York, 1941), p. 28.

113. *Ibid.,* p. 29.

114. *Ibid.,* p. 33. A recent example of how Spalding's name is associated with education in the public mind appeared in the *New York Times Magazine* of September 10, 1961, where an item entitled "Steps Along Paths of Learning," described as "a compendium of educated

101

comment on the timely subject of going to school," quoted twenty-three men, including Milton, Emerson, and Carlyle. Among these was Spalding, who was quoted as follows: "If education did nothing more than to open the great and vital books, giving us the ability to read ourselves into and out of them, the worth were beyond all price" (p. 66).

115. "The Higher Education," *Means and Ends of Education* (Chicago, 1909), p. 192.

116. Mt. 5:14–16.

117. *Ceremonies of the Golden Sacerdotal Jubilee . . .* , p. 17.

INDEX

Abbeloos, Jean B., and Catholic University of Louvain, 47

Alzog, Johann Baptist, 17

American College, at Louvain, 9 f; Spalding's attendance at, 10 ff

Apostolic Delegation, establishment of, 70

Archbishops, U. S., meeting (1892) regarding school controversy, 68 f

Belgium, Church and State in, 13 f

Bennett Law, in Wisconsin, 55

Blaine, James G., and public funds to religious education, 52

Blanchet, Francis Norbert, Archbishop, 23

Caldwell, Mary Gwendolen, gift to Catholic University of America, 38, 44

Catholic Educational Exhibit, World's Columbian Exposition (1893), 82 f

Catholic University of America, 23 ff; silver jubilee, 49 f; Spalding's efforts toward, 32–51 passim; Spalding's sermon at cornerstone laying, 42 ff

Catholic University of Louvain, opened, 7, 9

Church and State, in the United States, Spalding's views concerning, 71 f

Church of the Gesù, Spalding's speech at, 73 ff

Clergy, training of, 77 f

Columbia University, New York, presentation of honorary degree to Spalding, 84 f

Cooke, Jay, bank failure, 32

Corrigan, Michael A., Archbishop, 45

Curti, Merle, on Spalding's educational achievements, 86 ff

De Néve, John, and American College, at Louvain, 37 f

Education, as answer to nation's problems, Spalding's views on, 98 f, n. 69; in Peoria (Diocese) under Spalding, 28 ff; Spalding's views concerning, 51–70 passim, 74 f

"Education and the Future of Religion," Spalding's Roman sermon, 78

Edwards, Richard, and minimum education in Illinois, 54 ff

Elder, William Henry, Archbishop, and plans for a Catholic university, 32 f

Episcopal consecration, of Spalding, 51

Episcopal silver jubilee, of Spalding, 2

Essays and Reviews, 27, 51, 98, n. 66

Europe, Spalding's views concerning, 72 f

Faribault-Stillwater School Plan, 65 ff

Feehan, Patrick A., Archbishop, pastoral letter regarding education, 57 ff

Fisher, John, Saint, *see* John Fisher, Saint

Flaget, Benedict Joseph, Bishop, 7

Foley, Thomas, Bishop, co-consecrator of Spalding as bishop, 28

Freedom, intellectual, 75–77

Freiburg, University of, Spalding's attendance at, 17

Gabriels, Henry, Bishop, 95, n. 15

Gibbons, James Cardinal, 2; and Catholic University of America, 35 f; co-consecrator of Spalding as bishop, 28; speaker at silver jubilee, Catholic University of America, 50; speech to the National Education Association (1889), 62

Gilmour, Richard, Bishop, 37

Glennon, John J., Archbishop, regarding Spalding's career as educator, 90 f

Golden sacerdotal jubilee, celebrated by Spalding, 1 f, 49

Hennessy, Patrick, 36

Holy Cross College, Washington, D. C., Spalding's speech at dedication, 71 ff

Hovre, Franz de, on Spalding's educational achievements, 85 f

Illinois State Teachers Association, Spalding's speech to, 64

Ireland, John, Archbishop, speech to National Education Association (1890), 62 f

Irish Catholic Colonization Association, 30 ff

John Fisher, Saint, and curriculum at Christ's College, Cambridge, 97, n. 59

Journal (Peoria, Illinois) Spalding's correspondence regarding the school question, 58 ff

Katholischer Vereinsbund von Illinois, organized, 99, n. 74

Keane, John J., Archbishop, and Catholic University of America, 47, 48; speech to National Education Association (1889), 62

Kenrick, Francis Patrick, Archbishop, 9, 17

Lavialle, Peter J., Bishop, consecration, 18

Lebanon, Kentucky, birthplace of Spalding, 2

Lectures and Discourses, published, 35, 96, n. 46

Lefevere, Peter P., Bishop, 7

Leo XIII, Pope, *Testem benevolentiae,* 73

Louisville, Kentucky, Spalding's assignments in, 22

McCloskey, John, Cardinal, consecrator of Spalding as bishop, 28

McCloskey, William G., Bishop, 18

McQuaid, Bernard J., Bishop, and Catholic University of America, 36 f

Martinelli, Sebastiano, O.S.A., 71

Mount Saint Mary's College, Emmitsburg, Spalding's attendance at, 4 ff

Mount Saint Mary's of the West, Cincinnati, Spalding's attendance at, 8

Muldoon, Peter J., Bishop, 1

National Education Association, speeches by Gibbons, Keane, and Ireland to, 62 f

New World (Chicago) Catholic newspaper established, 57

New York City, Spalding's assignments in, 27 f

Ordination, of Spalding, 14, 16

Peoria, Illinois (Diocese) Spalding's appointment as bishop to, 28

Pius IX, Pope, *Quanta cura* and *Syllabus of Errors,* published, 19

Purcell, Edward, banking business failure, 32

Purcell, John B., Archbishop, 7

Religious Mission of the Irish People and Catholic Colonization, The, published, 31

Research, historical, Spalding's views concerning, 75

Riordan, Patrick W., Archbishop, 95, n. 15

Rome, Spalding's study in, 18 ff

Rosecrans, Sylvester H., Bishop, 8

Russell, David, first American student at American College at Louvain, 94, n. 13

Ryan, John A., on Spalding's achievements, 88 f

Saint Mary's College, Lebanon, Kentucky, Spalding's attendance at, 4

Satolli, Francesco, Archbishop, visit to United States regarding the school question, 67 ff

Schell, Brother Maurelian, F.S.C., 82

School controversy, 53 ff

Scripture, study of, 76

Seghers, Charles J., Archbishop, 95, n. 20

Shahan, Thomas J., Bishop, at Spalding's golden sacerdotal jubilee, 49

Shields, Thomas E., and the establishment of Sisters College, 81 f

Sisters College, Catholic University of America, establishment of, 82

Smith, Bernard, O.S.B., 18

Spalding, John Lancaster, Bishop, 1–91

Spalding, Martin John, Archbishop, 6 ff; appointed Archbishop of Baltimore, 17; biography of, by his nephew, 25, 27 f

Spalding, Mary Jane Lancaster (mother), 2 f

Spalding, Richard Martin (father), 2

Sterckx, Englebert, Cardinal, 9; leadership of, 12 ff

Taylor, Sister Euphrasia, establishment of Trinity College, Washington, D. C., 80

Testem benevolentiae (papal letter), 73

Trinity College, Washington, D. C., establishment of, 72, 80 f

Ubaghs, Casimir, controversy, 15

University of Freiburg, Spalding's attendance at, 17

Western Reserve University, Cleveland, presentation of honorary degree to Spalding, 84

Women, education of, 72, 74, 79 ff

World's Columbian Exposition, Catholic Educational Exhibit (1893), 56 f, 82 f